Victory in Europe

Endpapers US 17th
Airborne Division prepares
for the Rhine drop, March
1945

British, Soviet and
American flags flying over
Dachau concentration
camp after its liberation,
April 1945.

25 April 1945: General Emil
Reinhardt and General
Vladimir Rusakov lead the
celebrations as the

VICTORY IN EUROPE

D-DAY TO V-E DAY

MAX HASTINGS

PHOTOGRAPHS BY
GEORGE STEVENS

INTRODUCTION BY
GEORGE STEVENS, JR.

LITTLE, BROWN AND COMPANY
BOSTON   TORONTO

The publishers wish to thank the following for permission to
reproduce extracts from material to which they hold the copyright:

Brenda McBryde   *A Nurse's War* Brenda McBryde
Chatto & Windus, London

AJP Taylor   *The Second World War, An Illustrated
Hamish Hamilton, London   History* AJP Taylor
Atheneum Publishers, New York

Secker & Warburg, London   *Typhoon Pilot* Desmond Scott
(a Leo Cooper Book)

The publishers apologize for any omissions to this list.

First published in Great Britain by
George Weidenfeld & Nicolson Limited

Library of Congress Catalog Card No. 85–50176.

Book-of-the-Month Records® offers a wide range of
opera, classical and jazz recordings. For information
and catalog write to BOMR, Camp Hill, PA 17012.

CONTENTS

Introduction

When my father died in 1975 he left a storeroom in North Hollywood, California, where he had carefully maintained the evidence of his life. In that room I found letters, books, diaries, business records, awards, photographs, motion pictures and other things he had accumulated over the years.

He once said to me, 'If something happens to me, don't let that stuff in storage become a burden to you the way it has to me.' I know now what he meant. That storeroom contained thousands of intriguing documents and objects, and, today, nearly a decade after his death, I have not yet examined it all.

My father was a film director so it was not surprising to find one corner of the room filled with cans of film. Many were 35mm prints of his feature films, including *Alice Adams*; *Swing Time*; *Gunga Din*; *Woman of the Year*; *Shane*; *A Place in the Sun*; *Giant*; *The Diary of Anne Frank*; and *The Greatest Story Ever Told*. There were also 16mm films taken on movie sets, fishing trips and at family gatherings. On one shelf under an old army blanket were fourteen rusty cans with handwritten labels such as 'D-Day'; 'St Lô'; 'Paris-Liberation'; 'Russians-Torgau'; 'Duben to Dachau'; 'Potsdam-Berlin.' Over the years he and I had talked about this film, but, so far as I know, except for one brief, unsettling look at the Dachau reel, he never screened it.

One day after his death I took those rusty cans to the American Film Institute and asked the projectionist to run one of the reels. I sat alone in the small theatre, the lights went down and before me, in vivid colour, were scenes of ships at sea. I saw men in battle gear on the decks of what I would learn later was the HMS Belfast; next a flotilla of ships under barrage balloons as far as the eye could see; next 6-inch guns firing in the early morning light. In a close-up I saw my father raise his helmet as he peered through the lens of a motion picture camera. The reel ended with a shot of my father climbing into a landing craft bound for the Normandy shore where he, like so many others that day, would set foot on French soil for the first time.

This was D-Day *in colour*. I sat alone looking at incredibly luminous

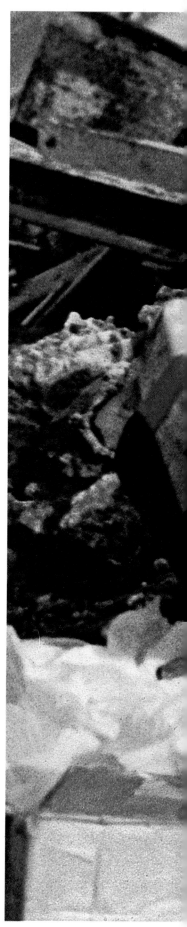

Christmas 1944, near
Bastogne. George Stevens
with a present from his son.

images of men and events as they were on 6 June 1944. And I realized that I was seeing views that had heretofore been seen only by the men who were part of that greatest seaborne invasion in history.

These films of D-Day and the five hours of other footage in this collection are, according to authorities at the Imperial War Museum in London and the National Archives in Washington, unique and virtually the only colour films of the war in Western Europe.

My father was George Stevens. He left Hollywood in 1942 to serve overseas in the American Army for three years in North Africa and Europe. General Eisenhower had been disappointed with the film record of the war, so Major, later Lieutenant-Colonel, Stevens was given orders to organize high-quality motion picture coverage of the forthcoming campaigns to free Europe from the Nazis.

In 1943 he began assembling SPECOU, the Special Coverage Unit of the U.S. Army Signal Corps. It became known variously as 'the Stevens Unit' or 'the Hollywood Irregulars'. Its members included crack cameramen, sound men, assistant directors and writers from the film industry. SPECOU was attached directly to SHAEF, the Supreme Headquarters Allied Expeditionary Force. The unit had official orders that enabled my father to assign small camera teams to move from army to army covering the major events of the war. Novelist Irwin Shaw, playwright William Saroyan and future screenwriter Ivan Moffat were responsible for writing captions and descriptions for the 35mm black-and-white film that the unit shot across Europe.

Army procedures called for all official motion picture coverage to be photographed in 35mm black-and-white, presumably because this was the standard for newsreels shown in movie theatres around the world, and because 35mm colour film existed only in the costly Technicolor process which called for three strips of film running simultaneously through a huge camera – not a likely device for a mobile army unit covering combat. That is why, today, when we envision the Second World War, we see a black-and-white war.

From the time he was a child my father took pictures. He started his

career as a camera assistant in Hollywood and when he was twenty-three became cameraman for Laurel and Hardy. I can't remember his presence at any one of my birthday parties without a 16mm home movie camera in hand. This instinct carried over to his army life. He carried a 16mm camera and Kodachrome film with him throughout the war, compiling a personal diary of the adventures of his unit.

I asked his friend and wartime comrade, Ivan Moffat, why he would add to the burdens of combat life by hauling along this extra equipment. His answer was simple: 'George was an observer of everything in life and all his instincts were for recording it. He was, after all, a film director.'

During 1944 and 1945 he, and the other men who rode with him in his jeep, would hand the camera back and forth, capturing their experiences. Periodically, he would send rolls of exposed colour film home to Hollywood for processing. Kodachrome, the film stock used for home movies, has no negative, as such. The exposed film is developed in the Eastman Kodak laboratory and returned as a print. Fortunately, Kodachrome film of that era had excellent dyes and the colour in these prints, unlike that in many feature films, has retained its quality through the decades.

This celluloid record of those times has been resting in storage for forty years. Why was it not shown earlier? I believe the answer can be found in the nature of George Stevens. He was a man who lived in the present. Although the Second World War was a central experience in his life – perhaps the most important to him – he had lived it and was not inclined to burrow back into old films and diaries to live it again. He was also a private man who saw his service in those years as his duty to his country. I suspect he regarded this diary of his unit as a personal record and that to exhibit it would be to publicize the performance of a civic duty. At the same time, he had a deep fascination with the course of human history and the tracks and traces left by earlier generations. He was a collector of the albums of the great Civil War photographer, Mathew Brady, so perhaps he hoped that someday these films would be uncovered and add something to the evidence of the mid-twentieth-century war to free Europe.

Lieutenant-Colonel George Stevens received the Legion of Merit from General Eisenhower for 'exceptional meritorious conduct', and the men of his unit were cited early in 1945 for 'work that has been both brilliant and outstanding, and accomplished for the most part under hazardous conditions, and has established a precedent and model for future campaign photography.'

The motion picture film they shot forms a large part of the black-and-white historical record of the Second World War. I know that with the publication of these colour enlargements from my father's 16mm diary of the Special Coverage Unit, he would wish that this volume be dedicated to his friends and colleagues of those years – the officers and men of SPECOU.

George Stevens, Jr.
Washington, D.C.

George Stevens' film unit in London before D-Day in 1944. *First row, left to right* Tom Henry, Norton McMillan, David Mott, Jack Muth, William Hamilton, Hal Lee, Forrest Weller, Ken Marthey, John Hines; *second row* Gordon Bush, Russell Day, Curtis Albertson, Pinkney Ridgell, Sandy Brooke, Andrew McCarthy, Phil Drell, Dick Kent; *third and fourth rows* Irwin Shaw, Ivan Moffat, Leicester Hemingway, Henry Moritz, Lieutenant Branham, Captain Reis, Captain Starling, Colonel Jervy, Lieutenant Morse, Major Stevens, Captain Mellor, Lieutenant Biroc, Lieutenant Montague, Lieutenant Herman, Lieutenant Johnson.

Overlord

'What Philip of Spain failed to do, what Napoleon tried and failed to do, what Hitler never had the courage to attempt, we are about to do' (Commander Rich). A panoramic view of the 5,339 vessels that were engaged in the largest amphibious operation ever undertaken in military history. In the background LSTs (Landing Ship, Tank) can be seen moving towards Juno Beach with small LCTs (Landing Craft, Tank) in the foreground, both protected overhead by barrage balloons.

The Allied invasion fleet crossing from England to Normandy kept to twelve narrow lanes in order to avoid minefields. From the starboard bridge wing of HMS Belfast, flagship of Force E, a line of three Royal Navy cruisers can be seen in the morning gloom.

IN THE early hours of 6 June 1944, preceded by airborne assaults to secure their flanks, the Allied armies landed on the beaches of Normandy to begin Operation Overlord, the struggle for North-West Europe. The American troops quickly gained a secure foothold on their western Utah Beach. Further east at Omaha, facing unexpectedly strong German defences dug into hillside positions, the US 1st and 29th Divisions suffered heavy casualties for the first few hours and seemed in danger of repulse. But by nightfall they had painfully cleared the bluffs covering the beaches, and were established just inland. Further east, on the three British and Canadian beaches – Gold, Juno and Sword – the invaders met less heavy resistance. But the German defenders were successful in achieving all that Field-Marshal Erwin Rommel, their commander, could reasonably have expected of them: they imposed sufficient check upon the attack to deprive General Sir Miles Dempsey's British Second Army of the momentum to gain its objective, the city of Caen, on that first day. The massive traffic jams of landing craft, tanks, vehicles and wreckage that built up along the tideline under spasmodic shellfire during the first vital hours after H-hour caused movement inland to fall behind schedule. The only significant German counter-attack of the day, by 21st Panzer Division against the British 3rd Division north-west of Caen, was decisively defeated. But it proved impossible to concentrate sufficient forces to push through the city by nightfall. As darkness fell on 6 June, all along the Normandy coast, Allied troops were digging foxholes, dozing over their weapons at positions in ditches and hedges, brewing up beside their tanks and vehicles. Their opponents, meanwhile, reeling beneath the massive shock that they had endured, struggled through the night to regroup shattered units and move forward reinforcements, creating a tenuous perimeter to contain the

A close-up view of a Royal Navy gun crew wearing anti-flash protective clothing on the quarter deck of HMS Belfast.

The 6-inch guns on the X and Y gun turrets of HMS Belfast light up the sky as they pound German positions ashore.

On Juno Beach. Allied troops pick their way through the traffic jam of landing craft and military equipment.

invasion beachhead. The Allies had gained a great strategic triumph, achieving absolute surprise and putting ashore 176,000 men in the first twenty-four hours of their landings to secure a foothold in North-West Europe.

The achievement of D-Day was not merely military; it also represented the culmination of a great political debate within the Grand Alliance. For the first eighteen months after their absolute defeat in France in May 1940, followed by their retreat from Dunkirk, the British were entirely preoccupied with their own struggle for survival. Their campaign in North Africa against the Italians and later against Rommel's Afrika Korps remained a sideshow, involving small forces by comparison with the great armies battering each other into ruin in other theatres of the Second World War. Even when Hitler invaded Russia in June 1941, for months it was assumed in the West that Stalin's defeat was inevitable. Reason decreed that Britain could do nothing to threaten Hitler's command of Europe. Only with the coming of winter did the first glimmer of hope dawn that the Red Army might, at the very least, inflict crippling damage on the Wehrmacht.

But from the moment the United States entered the war in December 1941, America's leaders began to press the British for an early invasion of France. Characteristic American directness of approach was matched by naïveté about the power of the German army, and the difficulty of defeating it. Washington was also haunted by fear of an imminent Russian collapse unless the Anglo-American armies could mount at least a diversion in the West. On the British side, there was much wisdom about the problems of mounting an invasion, yet also a reluctance to embark upon a bloody showdown with the Germans which persisted even when the huge resources required to make this realistic became available. The British were slow to grasp what the vast industrial power of the United States could achieve, and their repeated defeats at Hitler's hands had made them wary of staking everything upon one great throw. They preferred instead to gnaw at the weaker points in the crust of the Nazi empire: by fighting in the Mediterranean, threatening the Balkans, raiding the European coastline, supporting resistance movements, and above all bombing the cities and industries of Germany. After fighting for more than two years, and bearing the brunt of the struggle for two more, Britain and her leaders felt old, weary, impoverished of money and men. Their principal ambition, once it became apparent that the Allies could no longer lose the war, was to gain a victory at tolerable cost, preserving all that could be saved of Britain's pre-war greatness and worldwide possessions, and of her peoples' lives.

But after the British success at the Casablanca conference in January 1943, where Roosevelt and the American Chiefs-of-Staff were persuaded by Churchill to agree to the invasion of Sicily and the pursuit of a campaign into Italy, the United States' patience was at an end. General George Catlett Marshall, US Army Chief-of-Staff, and his

DUKWs or 'ducks' were amphibious cargo-carrying lorries, indispensable to the successful build-up of men and *matériel* on the Allied beachheads in Normandy. This example, seen moving inland from Juno Beach near St Aubin, is manned by 633 GT Company of the Royal Army Service Corps.

colleagues were unalterably determined that there should be an invasion of North-West Europe in 1944. Even into the winter of 1943, as the great Allied build-up in Britain continued, the British Chiefs-of-Staff sought to leave open a window for postponement of the invasion if conditions did not seem right. Churchill, and the Chief of the Imperial General Staff Sir Alan Brooke, did not dispute that sooner or later the Germans must be fought in North-West Europe. They were merely haunted by fear of the consequences of failure, or, almost more terrible, of a bloody stalemate in France resembling the campaign of

A Sherman flail minesweeping tank, one of the many ingenious devices invented by the British to overcome the defences of the Nazi Atlantic Wall, seen here behind Juno Beach in service with a 79th Armoured Division unit, the 22nd Dragoons. This Sherman flail tank appears to have been disabled by a landmine.

Right a close-up view of the British crew members.

thirty years before. 'My dear friend,' Churchill wrote to Roosevelt in October 1943, 'this is much the greatest thing we have ever attempted.' He cabled in like mood to Marshall in Washington: 'We are carrying out our contract, but I pray God it does not cost us dear.'

But the absolute single-mindedness of the Americans, and knowledge of the huge resources now available to throw against the German army, prevailed. D-Day was scheduled for 1 May, but was postponed to 5 June to make more landing craft available. General Dwight Eisenhower was named as Supreme Allied Commander, with

General Montgomery as land force commander for the initial invasion. More than 7,000 ships and 13,000 aircraft were to take part in the landings, with a million men going ashore in the first few weeks.

Although the attention of history has focussed most closely upon the great drama of 6 June as 'the longest day', from the outset the Allied planners believed that getting ashore would not be intolerably difficult, provided that the vital secret could be kept: where the invasion was to take place. Hitler's forces, under the overall leadership of Field-Marshal Gerd von Rundstedt and the local direction of Rommel, commanding Army Group B, were disposed along the entire Channel coast and deep inside France. The brilliant success of the Allied deception plan, Operation Fortitude, was that it kept the Germans in doubt, even weeks after D-Day, about the possibility of further Allied landings in the Pas de Calais. Throughout the war, German intelligence was one of the weakest links in Hitler's armour.

An ambulance launch comes alongside HMS Belfast with a casualty.

The casualty is winched amidships on the starboard side.

Members of the crew pull the soldier on board ship.

His armies possessed nothing to match the priceless Ultra decrypting operation of the Allies, which reaped a daily harvest of Germany's most secret signals traffic. As the war progressed and the certainty of defeat loomed larger and larger in the consciousness of Hitler's generals, a note of hysteria crept into their decisions and actions, most vividly reflected in the scores of high-ranking suicides in the last year. Rommel's drive and energy did much to strengthen the German defences on the Channel coast in the spring of 1944. But nothing could change the reality that Germany was seeking to defend all France with fifty-eight divisions, most of them miserably understrength,

The D-Day landings. At 6.30 am on 6 June 1944, the first waves of Allied forces reached the beaches of Normandy.

while the bulk of the Wehrmacht fought its doomed struggle of attrition in the East. Hitler was correct in believing that the will and confidence of his legendary general had been deeply corroded by pessimism. 'If I were doing the invasion,' Rommel told his staff laconically one morning before D-Day, 'I should be at the Rhine in fourteen days.'

The Allied organization and preparation for D-Day were the greatest logistical achievements in the history of warfare: the accumulation and transport of thousands of tons of stores, the movement of hundreds of thousands of men and their equipment, the gathering of the great seaborne armada. One outstanding victory had been won before D-Day began: the Allies gained absolute air superiority over North-West Europe. The bomber offensive had been frustrated in its hopes of destroying German aircraft in their factories. But when the American Mustang long-range escort fighter was

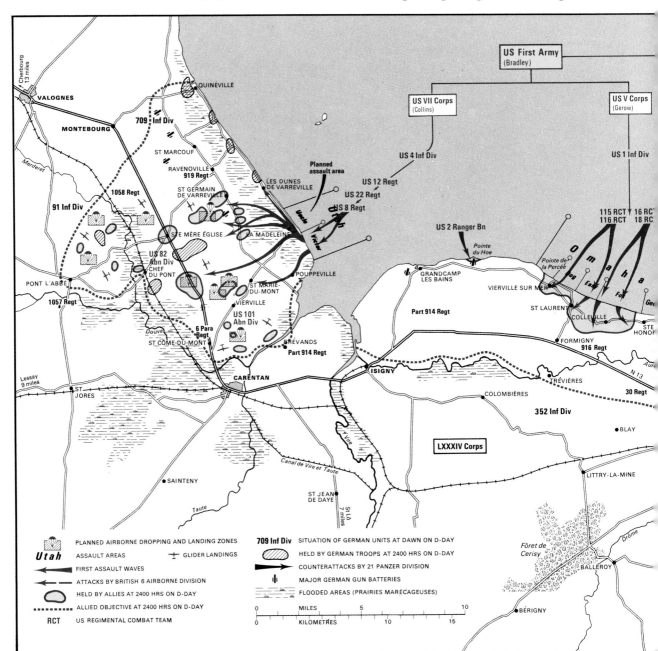

American GIs make themselves at home in the Normandy countryside; as this signpost shows, these soldiers were still closer to London than they were to Paris, their move forward in Normandy delayed by fierce German resistance.

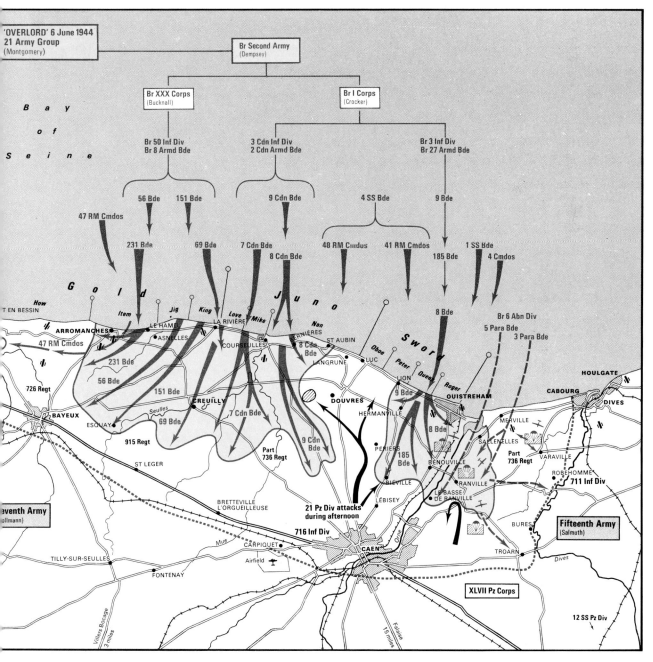

'OVERLORD' 6 June 1944
21 Army Group
(Montgomery)

Br Second Army
(Dempsey)

Br XXX Corps
(Bucknall)

Br I Corps
(Crocker)

Br 50 Inf Div
Br 8 Armd Bde

3 Cdn Inf Div
2 Cdn Armd Bde

Br 3 Inf Div
Br 27 Armd Bde

56 Bde   151 Bde

9 Cdn Bde

4 SS Bde

9 Bde

47 RM Cmdos

231 Bde   69 Bde

7 Cdn Bde
8 Cdn Bde

48 RM Cmdos   41 RM Cmdos

1 SS Bde   4 Cmdos
185 Bde

8 Bde

Br 6 Abn Div
5 Para Bde
3 Para Bde

Bay
of
Seine

Gold   Juno   Sword

How
T EN BESSIN

Item
ARROMANCHES
47 RM Cmdos
ASNELLES

Jig   King
LE HAMEL
LA RIVIÈRE

Love   Mike
CERNIERES
COURSEULLES
8 Cdn
Bde
LANGRUNE

Nan
ST AUBIN

Oboe   Peter
LUC
LION
Queen
Roger
9 Bde
OUISTREHAM

HOULGATE

CABOURG
DIVES

231 Bde
56 Bde
151 Bde

726 Regt
BAYEUX

CREUILLY

Seulles
69 Bde

ESQUAY

915 Regt

7 Cdn Bde

DOUVRES
HERMANVILLE

MERVILLE

SALLENELLES
Part
736 Regt
VARAVILLE

ROBEHOMME
711 Inf Div

8 Bde

PERIERS
185
Bde
BENOUVILLE
RANVILLE

9 Cdn
Bde

Part
736 Regt

ST LEGER

BRETTEVILLE
L'ORGUEILLEUSE

21 Pz Div attacks
during afternoon

716 Inf Div

BIÉVILLE
LÉBISEY
LE BASSE
DE RANVILLE

BURES

eventh Army
(ollmann)

TILLY-SUR-SEULLES

Mue
CARPIQUET
Airfield

FONTENAY

CAEN
Orne

TROARN

Dives

Fifteenth Army
(Salmuth)

XLVII Pz Corps

Villers Bocage
3 miles

Falaise
15 miles

12 SS Pz Div

The towns and villages of Normandy took a terrible battering from Allied artillery and bombers as these scenes show: *right* civilians share a road with a US Army GMC 2½ ton truck; *below* in this wrecked town the façade of the church appears to be the only building still standing.

launched into the skies over Germany in the first months of 1944, it achieved extraordinary success in destroying the Luftwaffe in the air. On D-Day, Göring's pilots proved able to fly a mere 319 sorties against the beachhead. In the months that followed they mounted only nuisance raids against the Allied armies. The RAF and USAAF, meanwhile, created critical difficulties for German reinforcements by devastating rail and bridge links to the battlefield, and each day flying thousands of tactical missions in support of the armies. The air forces' most extravagant convictions and promises – that unaided they could achieve victory for the Allies – merely diminished the credibility of their own commanders. But given the extraordinary power and skill of the German army, the Allied command of the skies was critical: 'The Anglo-American air forces did more than facilitate the historic invasion', wrote the American official historians. 'They made it possible.'

Allied troops entered Caen in early July, but by now Rommel had received heavy reinforcements. It was on 18 July that General Montgomery launched Operation Goodwood, which pinned down the German Panzer units around the British and Canadian sectors of the Allied beachhead in Normandy.

Coutances, which was liberated by the US First Army on 28 July 1944.

Much criticism was thrust upon Eisenhower during the war and after its conclusion for his failings as a soldier, and indeed even his admirers concede that he was no battlefield commander. Yet throughout the 1944–45 campaign, Eisenhower revealed a greatness of spirit as Supreme Commander and military leader of the Alliance which it is difficult to imagine being matched by another general. Nowhere was this seen to greater advantage than during the critical D-Day launching conferences of 3 and 4 June, when the weather seemed to threaten the fulfilment of all the Allies' hopes. Montgomery, in one of the major misjudgements of his career, urged that the landing should go ahead on 5 June. Given the difficulties that occurred in better weather on the 6th, it seems possible that disaster could have befallen the Allies had they gone ahead a day earlier. As it was, Eisenhower alone assumed the vast responsibility first, for postponing the invasion on the 5th and committing his vast force to another day of confinement on their ships; and second, for setting the invasion in motion, gambling hugely on the accuracy of Group-Captain Stagg's prediction of a weather 'window', on the 6th. 'I'm quite positive we must give the order', he said at the meeting at 9.45 pm on 4 June. 'I don't like it, but there it is ... I don't see how we can possibly do anything else.'

Thus the greatest amphibious force the world had ever seen began to steam its slow, ponderous course across the darkened Channel. Below decks thousands of men lay crammed in their bunks reading, sleeping, playing poker, nursing sea-sickness and the great tension thrust upon them by knowledge of what lay ahead. Above them in the night sky, the great fleet of transport aircraft and gliders droned towards its dropping zones packed with men, each one clumsily burdened by his deadweight of weapons and equipment. Resistance groups throughout France received the Action Messages for which they had waited so long, alerting them to mobilize and begin acting against German units and communications. Incredibly, even now the German High Command failed to perceive either the invasion fleet or the significance of the massive Allied activity. Rommel was absent in Germany for his wife's birthday. Many of his most senior commanders were away from their headquarters. Even when British and American parachutists began to pour down through the darkness upon Normandy and the Cotentin peninsula, the German response was bewildered and uncertain. That *a* landing was taking place was evident. That this was *the* landing, they failed for many days to understand.

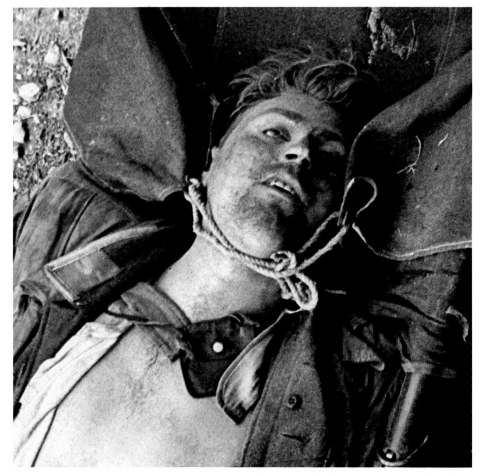

The Wehrmacht lost over a quarter of a million men in Normandy from D-Day to 25 August 1944.

The drop of the 82nd and 101st Airborne Divisions, the outstanding combat formations of the American army, was crippled by almost criminal carelessness and incompetence by the transport pilots, who scattered thousands of men throughout the Cotentin peninsula rather than on their scheduled dropping zones, and parachuted hundreds to instant death in marshes and flooded fields. But it was a tribute to the Americans' tenacity that wherever they landed, they began to fight. Their great contribution was to create chaos throughout the western sector of the German defences. They secured a narrow passage for the seaborne invaders moving inland from Utah Beach across causeways through the countryside deliberately flooded by the Germans. The British, in one of the great *coup de main* operations of the war, secured the bridges across the River Orne and the Caen Canal by a night glider landing, and created a perimeter eastward that the 6th Airborne Division defended with superb courage through the days that followed.

In the grey light of dawn, the astounded defenders of the coastline peered forth from their bunkers and pillboxes to see before them the Allied armada. The first waves of landing craft, packed with sodden men, bucketed towards the beaches through the surf amid the rippling flashes and explosions of fire from the great gunline of battleships, cruisers and destroyers covering the landings. The German coastal batteries began to reply, and their fire sank or damaged dozens of craft as they ran in. Some grounded offshore and began to offload men and tanks, only to see them plunge into deep water and prompt death.

Fallschirmjäger, German parachute troops, were among the toughest and most feared fighters in the German armies in Normandy. This picture shows one of the many thousands of casualties that the *Fallschirmjäger* regiments suffered against the US First Army.

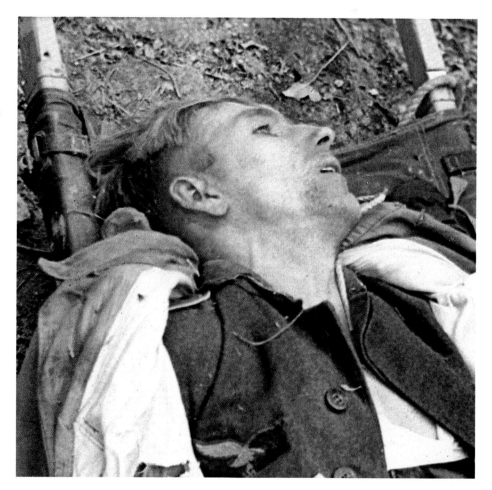

General Omar Bradley, whose US First Army captured St Lô on 19 July 1944 in some of the bitterest fighting to take place in North-West Europe.

Lieutenant-General George Patton, commander of the US Third Army which was to spearhead the Allied break-out from Normandy, is shown here with his famous pearl-handled pistol at the 21st Army Group's main headquarters at Creully. He shares a joke with Major-General Francis de Guingand (Montgomery's Chief-of-Staff), while Montgomery chats with a Lieutenant-Colonel of the Coldstream Guards.

Others drifted onto the beaches on fire or crewless, to burn all day at the waterline. Some men who had trained for four years for this moment died in the first seconds of the landings. Others lay wounded in shallow water, or huddled against beach obstacles, hampering the engineers working to destroy these before the next tide. Yet most, perhaps to their own surprise, survived the mortaring, the machine-guns, the mines, and pressed on up the beaches, through the ribbon of houses stretching along the coast behind the British beaches, to their concentration points inland. Gun tanks and specialized armour for mine-clearing, bridging and strongpoint demolition lumbered along-side the infantry, mopping up pockets of resistance. Some German positions behind the British beaches held out until nightfall and beyond, inflicting heavy casualties and critically delaying the advance inland. On Omaha Beach, the Americans had to fight their way off the beach yard by yard, clearing bunkers one by one. It was late

A rare picture of Ernest
Hemingway (*left*) who was
a war correspondent for
Collier's magazine during
the battle for France. *Right*
Oscar-winning cameraman,
Captain William Mellor.

The US First Army took
Cherbourg on 27 June 1944.
This picture shows the
townspeople celebrating
Bastille Day (14 July) with
their liberators.

afternoon before most of the beach exits were cleared for vehicles. At
Utah, where strong currents brought the landing craft ashore several
hundred yards south of their planned objectives, the landing force
thus gained an unexpectedly easy foothold. But strong German
positions further north remained intact, and became the scene of
fierce fighting in the days that followed.

Yet the Allies were ashore at a cost of only some 2,000 men killed, an
incomparably lighter price than they had expected to pay for so great a
prize. The battle for North-West Europe had been launched with a
brilliant beginning. In London *The Times* went to press that night
with a leading article that echoed the sense of triumph throughout the
West the next morning: 'Four years after the rescue at Dunkirk of that
gallant defeated army without which as a nucleus the forces of
liberation could never have been rebuilt, the United Nations returned
today with power to the soil of France.'

MOVING UP

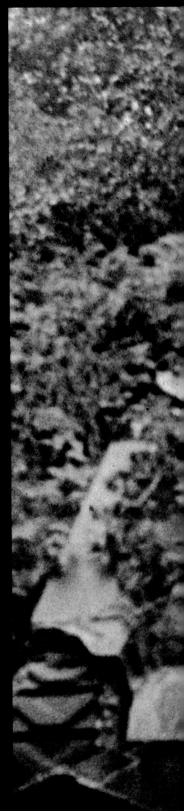

By late July the Allies had nearly two million troops in France and a quarter of a million vehicles. These pictures show: *far right* an M4 Sherman tank moving down a lane in *bocage* country with 'Rhino' prongs fitted to its bows. These prongs, constructed from salvaged German beach defences, were hurriedly fitted to American tanks before the start of Operation Cobra, designed to crack German resistance in the *bocage* prior to the breakout from the Normandy beachhead. 'Rhino' prongs enabled tanks to slice through the hedgerows which lined the country roads and thus gain quick mobility. *Top* an M4 Sherman tank fitted with a dozer blade, one attempt by the Allied armies to solve the problem of hedgerows but superceded

by the 'Rhino' prongs. *Above* an obsolete M3 Lee tank, converted into an armoured recovery vehicle (ARV) with a dummy 75mm gun as the main 'armament'.

The Battle for Normandy

A lorryload of lightly-guarded German prisoners being transported to a prison camp.

Relaxed-looking GIs moving up to the front in a GMC 2½ ton truck.

THE TOWERING suspense that hung over 6 June 1944 in the minds of the Allied High Command was born of their knowledge of the consequences of failure. Yet from the moment the plans were made, all military logic suggested that on D-Day the very best of the Allied armies would prevail over some of the least impressive elements of the Wehrmacht defending the coastline. Their greatest fears were concentrated upon what might happen in the weeks that followed, as the mass of the German army in the West, above all the SS Panzer divisions, reached the battlefield. 'I do not doubt our ability in the conditions laid down to get ashore and deploy', Churchill had written to Roosevelt the previous winter. 'I am however deeply concerned with the build-up and with the situation which may arise between the thirtieth and sixtieth days.' In June and July 1944, the battle for Normandy unfolded in a fashion which seemed to threaten fulfilment of the worst of Churchill's misgivings.

On 7 June the Allies gained Bayeux, and the Americans consolidated their positions around Omaha and Utah beachheads. Men and vehicles continued to pour ashore from the sea. The next day, British and American forces met near Port-en-Bessin. The Canadians successfully repulsed a series of ferocious counter-attacks by 12th SS Panzer Division, the most formidable and fanatical German formation to fight in Normandy. But in the days that followed, despite constant Allied air attacks on roads and railways, Rommel's armoured forces narrowly succeeded in creating a cordon around the Allied armies as they moved west and south to expand their beachhead. One by one, 21st Panzer Division, 12th SS Panzer, Bayerlein's great *Panzer Lehr*,

A local football ground outside St Lô in use as a temporary prison camp.

A GI gets a suntan while keeping watch on German prisoners with a Browning .5 machine-gun on an anti-aircraft mounting.

German prisoners looking relaxed and happy despite being held in captivity behind barbed wire.

and 2nd Panzer swung into line around the British and Canadian sector.

Further west, the Americans faced less formidable opposition, and very few German tanks. But fighting in the worst of the thickly-hedged *bocage* country, with many of their infantry units new to battle, undertrained and not notably well led, General Omar Bradley's divisions made slow progress towards cutting the Cotentin peninsula and making for the vital port of Cherbourg. For so many months, the thoughts of the Allied armies had focussed upon crossing the narrow strip of sand skirting Hitler's Atlantic Wall. Once they had done so, it was not surprising that they needed a breathing space, psychologically, to adjust to the new demands of the struggle beyond the beaches. But the price, for the Allied cause, was a sluggishness and caution about the armies' forward movement in those first vital days after 6 June, before the Germans reached the battlefield in strength. Key roads and towns lay open for the taking in the beginning. But once the German defences hardened, these same blossom-clad farmhouses and orchards, hamlets and hilltop villages, required weeks and much blood and misery to secure. Some of Montgomery's American critics sardonically contrasted his promises and demands before the invasion of lightning movement inland, with the reality of laboured progress. Yet responsibility for this extended down the entire Allied chain of command to platoon and squad level. It did not reflect any definable failure by Montgomery himself. Many Allied units were new to battle, and had to learn their business day by day in the hedges and fields of Normandy. Others, recalled from the Mediterranean to provide a stiffening of experience for the invasion forces, were weary after years of war, and proved reluctant, on the European battlefield, to recall the dash and sacrifice by which they had made their reputations.

By 12 June, the Allied armies were in continuous contact along a 50-mile perimeter. It had always been Montgomery's intention to present a 'strong shield' to the German armoured forces on his left, the Anglo-Canadian front, and thus to enable the Americans to carry out the 'breakout' on the right. It was inevitable that the Germans would rush their strongest forces to the defence of the eastern sector, so many miles closer to Paris and to the heart of Germany. But for all Montgomery's postwar claims that the battle progressed strictly to his plan, there is no doubt he wished that 'strong shield' to stand south of Caen, giving the armies elbow room in the beachhead, and space for vital airfield construction. In the weeks after D-Day, he mounted a series of major attacks in an effort to seize Caen head on, thereafter with the intention of enveloping the city. He abandoned the direct attack after his Second Army had suffered heavy casualties. It is often forgotten that more men died each day in the bitter fighting after D-Day than on D-Day itself. On 11 June, Montgomery sent his crack veteran 51st Highland Division to attack through 6th Airborne's hard-held positions east of the Orne. It was a deep disappointment to him when the Scots failed to gain their objectives, and he was compelled to break off this eastern attack: 'Regret to report . . . 51st Division is at present not – NOT – battleworthy', he cabled to Brooke afterwards, having sacked its commander. 'It does not fight with determination and has failed in every operation it has been given to do.'

But an even more serious failure now followed. West of Caen, Allied

The Wehrmacht was adept at sowing landmines and booby traps in the path of the advancing Allies in Normandy. This sequence, filmed in Coutances, shows first a jeep setting off a mine and GIs scattering to escape further explosions.

intelligence detected a gap in the German line, around the town of Villers-Bocage. Montgomery sent his 7th Armoured Division, the legendary 'Desert Rats', to secure this breach before German reinforcements could reach and close it. On 12 June, the division made slow progress against dogged German outpost resistance, exploiting the close country to use their anti-tank weapons. On the 13th, a tank regiment and infantry company in half-tracks at last worked through Villers-Bocage and halted along the open road beyond the town. In a field alongside, unseen by the British, were leaguered four Tiger tanks from an SS tank battalion newly arrived on the battlefield. To the astonishment and consternation of the Desert Rats, these now opened fire. One of them, commanded by Captain Michael Wittmann, the outstanding tank ace of the war, charged the stationary British line, firing as he advanced, and drove on into the main street of Villers-Bocage, destroying a helpless succession of 7th Armoured's Cromwell tanks. Before the Panzers withdrew, they wiped out the British infantry company and most of the armoured regiment.

Here troops approach the shattered jeep and *right* medics treat a badly injured GI.

Local German commanders, perceiving the critical importance of holding Villers-Bocage, now scraped together a rag-bag of available infantry, guns and rear area troops from nearby divisions, and pushed them towards the town under command of a staff officer. In the course of fierce fighting all that day, British infantry reinforcements destroyed several German tanks, including that of Wittmann. But by nightfall they were compelled to retreat. The following day, 7th Armoured pulled back towards Caumont under continuous German pressure. The battle for Villers-Bocage had been a startling demonstration of German speed, ruthlessness and professionalism. Above all, it highlighted the crippling weakness of Allied tanks – the Cromwells, Shermans and Churchills – against German Tigers, Panthers and Mark IVs whose armour most Allied tank guns could not penetrate. The official Washington and London view before D-Day was that some inferiority in the quality of Allied tanks was acceptable because of their vast quantitative superiority. Yet on the battlefield, again and again in North-West Europe, very small numbers of German

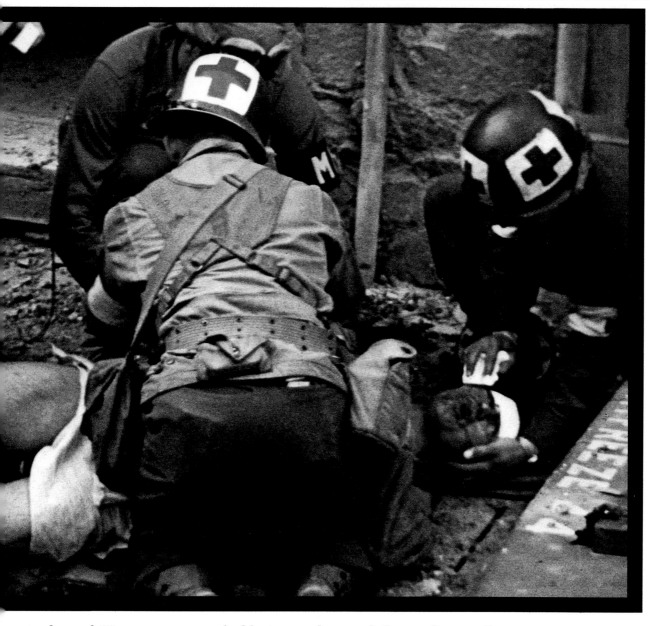

tanks and 88mm guns proved able to repulse much larger forces of Allied armour. Allied crews became justifiably cautious about pressing forward against Tigers and Panthers when they saw so many of their comrades 'brewed up' in the attempt.

When the Germans closed the gap in their line at Villers-Bocage, they completed a continuous perimeter around the Allies. Thenceforth, for more than two months, the Normandy campaign became a bloody 'slogging match', by its conclusion embracing more than two million men. Allied air power and ground strength prevented Rommel from launching a single major counter-attack. Yet the repeated failure of Allied assaults caused growing dismay and apprehension at the summit of the Grand Alliance. The invaders suffered a serious setback to their build-up in the 'Great Storm' which battered the Channel coast and the Normandy beaches from 19 to 21 June, costing 140,000 tons of scheduled stores and ammunition deliveries. On the 26th, the British Second Army launched a major attack on a four-mile front towards the thickly-wooded banks of the River Odon. Operation

Rather belatedly, a mine detector is brought into action.

Epsom, as it was called, made rapid initial progress, but then met heavy resistance. When at last British armour fought its way across the Odon and seized Hill 112 on 29 June, they were counter-attacked by 9th and 10th SS Panzer Divisions, newly-arrived from the Eastern Front. The Germans were repulsed. But General Dempsey believed his forces on Hill 112 were too battered to withstand further punishment. They withdrew across the Odon having suffered more than 4,000 casualties. On 30 June Epsom was closed down. Had the British but known it, their opponents were at that moment at the limits of their endurance. But Montgomery and his commanders were haunted, as they would be for the remainder of the war, by fear of heavy infantry casualties which could not be replaced. The British army relentlessly shrank in size through the months that followed, while that of the Americans vastly expanded.

Meanwhile, on the Western Front, the Americans at last gained Cherbourg on 27 June, and by the 30th control of the entire Cotentin peninsula. General J.Lawton 'Lightning Joe' Collins, commanding the US VII Corps, proved himself one of the outstanding leaders and drivers of men in Bradley's army during the battle for Cherbourg. But the prize his men had gained proved bitterly sour. It was discovered that before the port's fall, the Germans had conducted one of the most comprehensive demolition operations of the war. The Overlord logistics plan called for Cherbourg to receive 150,000 tons of stores by 25 July. Instead, by that date less than 18,000 tons had been offloaded. It was late September before the port approached full operational capacity. The drive for Cherbourg had thus failed to achieve its principal strategic purpose, and when the Americans renewed their attack southwards, they made slow progress through the *bocage*. 'Sometimes I wish I had George Patton over there', Eisenhower reflected moodily as he heard reports of the US First Army's difficulties.

For the men of the Allied armies fighting in Normandy, the summer beauty of the French countryside mocked their chronic fear and weariness. Each massive hedge was a natural defensive position from which German gunners fired unseen, and in which they could only be destroyed by a direct hit from a shell or bomb. The Allies sought to save the lives of their men in North-West Europe by blasting a path for each ground assault with thousands of tons of high explosives from warships, artillery and aircraft. Yet in Normandy, while this policy razed towns and villages to rubble, it proved astonishingly ineffective in crushing opposition. Rommel's men were dismayed by the weight of Allied resources deployed against them, yet they fought with a stubborn courage born of desperation. With the prospect of distant victory in sight, many Allied soldiers yearned to remain alive to see the moment, and much of Montgomery's popularity with his men was inspired by his determination to expend their lives sparingly. Their opponents, meanwhile, seemed possessed by the spirit of *götterdämmerung*. Though the German infantry battalions and tank regiments were being remorselessly ground down without hope of replacement, the remnants held their positions. Von Rundstedt and Rommel pleaded in vain with Hitler to be allowed to carry out a major strategic withdrawal, to enable them at least to fight out of range of Allied naval gunfire. Hitler, in his madness, insisted that every yard of France must be defended. Through those bloody summer weeks, Army Group B fought one of the great defensive actions of history, a battle which reflected no great genius or even intelligence by the German High Command, but immense skill and determination by the German soldier and his leaders at regimental level and below. The Allies suffered terribly in every attack. Just fourteen per cent of British troops in France were infantrymen, yet they bore more than three-quarters of the casualties. Eighty-four per cent of all American casualties were infantry, sixty-three per cent of these riflemen. It was not uncommon for rifle companies to lose thirty or forty per cent of their strength in a single attack. 'Battle fatigue' became a serious problem in the Allied armies, above all among the infantry, and notably in the American sector where, in the last weeks of June and the first of July, this condition reached epidemic proportions.

The western ruins of Caen were at last occupied by the British and Canadians on 9 July, after a massive bomber attack had levelled most of the city before them. The Germans continued, however, to hold

Pockets of German
resistance held out in
Brittany long after the US
advance had moved on.
Gunners from the US 83rd
Infantry Division are seen
in action here with a
captured German 15cm
self-propelled gun
bombarding German
positions on the tiny Ile de
Cézembre off St Malo on
18 August.

commanding observation positions in the south-eastern suburbs, and a renewed British effort to seize Hill 112 was frustrated by a German counter-attack, with heavy casualties. Early on the morning of 18 July, Montgomery mounted yet another major attack from the British sector. Although he later claimed that he sought only to 'write down' German forces and cherished no territorial ambitions, in reality there is no doubt that he hoped that Operation Goodwood – launched east of the Orne against the Bourguébus Ridge – would reach Falaise. This was a massed tank attack by 7th, 11th and Guards Armoured Divisions, for at this stage of the campaign the British felt able to sacrifice tanks in large numbers, but not infantry. Preceded by the now customary massed air bombardment, Goodwood started strongly. But then it ran into characteristically stubborn German resistance. From out of the bomb craters and wrecked vehicles and shattered villages, dazed defenders somehow roused themselves to man their tanks and 88mm guns. The British preparations for Goodwood had been obvious to the Germans, who had created defensive positions in extraordinary depth on the Bourguébus Ridge. This was, indeed, the last achievement of Rommel in command, for on 17 July he was

The shell bursts on its target.

seriously wounded by a strafing fighter-bomber, and replaced by Field-Marshal Günther Hans von Kluge, a dour veteran of the Eastern Front.

Goodwood only took part of the ridge. Unsupported massed tanks, attacking in daylight across open ground, were not a tactically sound method of breaking through the German positions, as some of those leading the assault feared before it began. Goodwood was closed down on 21 July, having cost the British 5,537 casualties and the loss of 400 tanks, thirty-six per cent of their total armoured strength in France. The tanks were readily replaced. But the damage to Anglo-American relations, and above all to the prestige of Montgomery, was never entirely repaired. For all the evidence that the overwhelming bulk of German strength was committed against the British, the Americans increasingly believed that Dempsey's Second Army was bearing less than its share of the Allied burden, and certainly achieving less than its promised share of success. In reality, it was Montgomery's grandiose promises and declarations, his rashness in seeking to ignore the feelings of Eisenhower and his deputy Air Chief Marshal Sir Arthur Tedder, which were largely responsible for the tensions within the Alliance, rather than any failure of generalship. The British, Canadians and Americans were attempting to defeat the outstanding fighting force of the Second World War. Even with massive Allied superiority of tanks, guns, air and sea power, the Germans could be broken only after a protracted, painful struggle of attrition. By late July von Kluge's formations were indeed on their knees. But understanding of the enemy's critical predicament dawned on the Allies too late to prevent a bitter wrangle within the High Command. Churchill's patience was waning, the terrible fear of stalemate haunting his thoughts. Eisenhower was being compelled to endure much criticism from America, where it was alleged that the Anglo-Americans preferred to leave the Russians to win the war. Military and political tensions at the summit of the Alliance threatened to break into open conflict, but the situation was dramatically transformed by victory.

The breakthrough on the American front, when it came, developed with bewildering speed. On 25 July 1944, Collins's VII Corps, supported by General Charles Corlett's XIX and General T.H. Middleton's VIII Corps jumped off for Operation Cobra, south from the Periers-St Lô road. They faced only the ruins of *Panzer Lehr* and a few shrunken German battle groups. On the first day, even these caused severe difficulties for the Americans. But thereafter, Bradley's divisions raced southwards meeting negligible resistance. They reached Avranches on 30 July, and thence turned the 'elbow' into Brittany. Here, General George Patton's Third Army was activated, and it was Patton who led the exhilarating rush west, pursuing fleeing German units as they sought refuge in the fortified Brittany ports of Brest, Lorient and St Nazaire. General Paul Hausser's Seventh Army disintegrated. Though the Americans fought some bitter battles against fragments of shattered units, cutting their way eastward, the entire left of the German line in France had collapsed. In the first days of August, the American XV Corps wheeled east towards Le Mans, while XX Corps drove south for the Loire.

The American dash across Brittany arguably diverted the critical

Canadian soldiers in a Bren-gun carrier under camouflage netting, guarding a captured German airfield at Carpiquet, outside Caen, during July 1944.

burden of their strength from the east, when the Germans might still have achieved a measured withdrawal to the Seine. 'Whether the enemy can still be stopped at this point is questionable', the desperate von Kluge reported to Hitler. 'The enemy air superiority is terrific, and smothers almost every one of our movements.' But the Führer's insane strategic delusions now ensured the destruction of his army in France. Against the passionate advice of his generals, he insisted that an armoured counter-attack should be launched westward through Mortain, aiming to cut the American line at Avranches. On 7 July, almost every surviving German armoured unit in Normandy was committed to battle on the Mortain front against the American 30th and 9th Divisions. It was a measure of the Americans' growing confidence and professionalism that, forewarned by Ultra about German intentions, they responded coolly and decisively to the

Mortain assault. Isolated American units fought with great determination until they were relieved three days later. American tanks and fighter-bombers crushed the German assaults with devastating losses. By the night of 12 August, the Germans were in full retreat, having lost most of their remaining armour in the West. The American XV Corps reached Argentan on the 13th, holding up the promise of encircling the entire German army in Normandy. Patton made his legendary demand to Bradley: 'We have elements in Argentan. Shall we continue and drive the British into the sea for another Dunkirk?'

For American impatience with the British was heightened by their absence from Argentan that very day. On 6 August, Montgomery had nominated the town as the boundary between the Americans advancing from the south and the Anglo-Canadian forces moving from the north. Here, he hoped, the Germans would be entrapped in a sealed pocket between the converging Allied armies. Yet while Bradley's armies dominated the headlines of the world with their great sweep across north-west France, their allies were advancing painfully slowly towards Falaise, gaining ground yard by yard. At last, the bulk of German forces had shifted west to face the Americans. Yet when the Canadians launched Operation Totalize on the night of 7 August, the fanatical remnants of 12th SS Panzer proved capable of halting them almost unaided. The attack bogged down on the night of 9 August. German tank strength on the Canadian front was reduced to 35, against 700 in the Canadian II Corps alone. Yet it was decided that only another full-scale set-piece assault would enable the Canadian First Army to proceed. This new operation, code-named Tractable, opened under a massive smokescreen on the morning of 14 August, and cleared Falaise only on the 17th. Thereafter, the Poles and Canadians spearheading the advance were directed to pivot eastward towards the village of Trun, extending their reach in the hope that they might still trap the German army, now in full retreat. Yet Canadian progress remained slow. The Poles fought a desperate battle at Mont Ormel against German armour struggling to hold open the escape route east. American and Canadian forces did not complete a secure junction until 20 August, when at last the 'Falaise pocket' was sealed. More than 40,000 of the most fanatical elements of the German army had escaped east towards the Seine, to fight another day in the defence of their Fatherland.

Yet the ruin of Army Group B in the Falaise pocket was almost complete. The victors counted 344 German tanks and self-propelled guns, 2,447 soft-skinned vehicles and 252 guns either destroyed or abandoned. The battle for Normandy had cost the Germans around 450,000 casualties (240,000 of these killed or wounded), 1,500 tanks, 3,500 guns and 20,000 vehicles. Forty German divisions had been destroyed at a cost of 209,672 Allied casualties, 36,976 of these killed. Von Kluge himself died by his own hand on 17 August, on the way home to Germany in disgrace, suspected of treachery to Hitler. Field-Marshal Walther Model inherited his command, in time only to preside over the salvage of the wreckage of the German armies in France. For all the Allied recriminations and heart-searching about their slow progress from the sea, Hitler's manic insistence upon reinforcing failure, feeding division after division into the cauldron rather than yield ground, vastly increased the magnitude of German defeat when it came. The wrangle about the delay in closing the Falaise Gap was overdone. Although the inability of the Canadians to fulfil Montgomery's proclaimed intention was an embarrassment to him, there is every reason to suppose that if the Allies had blocked the eastward escape of the German army with a north–south cordon around 15 August, the Germans would have smashed through it. At that stage, they were fighting everywhere with the ferocity of desperate men. As it was, their retreat was harassed ceaselessly by artillery fire and fighter-bomber attack. One of the RAF's Typhoon pilots, Group-Captain Desmond Scott, took a jeep to view the carnage to which he had contributed at Falaise, to see the debris of Hitler's doomed attempt to stem the breaches made on 6 June in the Atlantic Wall of his empire:

'The roads were choked with wreckage and the swollen bodies of men and horses. Bits of uniforms were plastered to shattered tanks and trucks and human remains hung in grotesque shapes on the blackened hedgerows. Corpses lay in pools of dried blood, staring into space as if their eyes were being forced from their sockets. Two grey-clad bodies, both minus their legs, leaned against a clay bank as if in prayer. I stumbled over a typewriter. Paper was scattered around where several mailbags had exploded. I picked up a photograph of a smiling young German recruit standing between his parents, two solemn peasants

As Patton's Third Army overran Brittany, Allied troops forced the German opposition into a pocket between Falaise and Argentan.

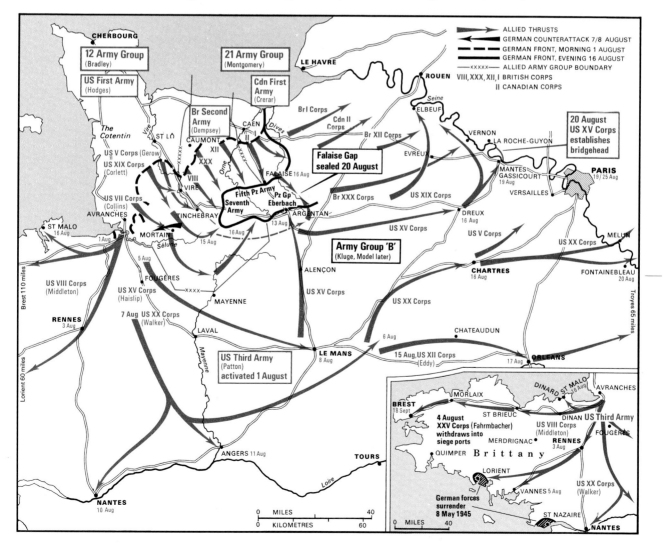

who stared back at me in accusation ... Strangely enough it was the fate of the horses that upset me most. Harnessed as they were, it had been impossible for them to escape, and they lay dead in tangled heaps, their large wide eyes crying out to me in anguish. It was a sight that pierced the soul, and I felt as if my heart would burst. We did not linger, but hurried back to the sanctity of our busy airfield near Bayeux.'

A Wehrmacht corporal of the 276th Infantry Division, who escaped on foot to the Seine with a handful of other stragglers from the ruin of his unit, said simply: 'After Normandy, we had no illusions any more. We knew that we stood with our backs to the wall.'

French civilians present flowers to George Stevens and Irwin Shaw after the liberation of Coutances by US troops.

CHAPTER THREE

Liberation

French civilians became soldiers overnight. The FFI (*Forces Françaises de l'Intérieur*) quickly armed themselves with small arms and grenades. This Frenchman holds a British-made Sten gun.

Some of the FFI were able to combine glamour with fire power, this time a captured MP 40 or *Schmeisser* sub-machine gun, a much-prized weapon among Allied troops.

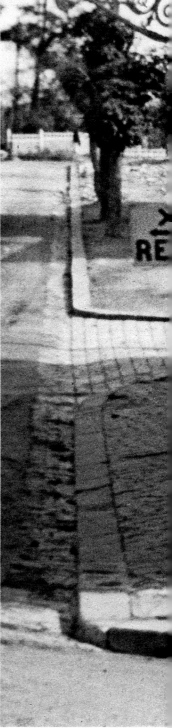

SINCE 6 JUNE 1944, all over France thousands of French *résistants* had been under arms: skirmishing or fighting bloody battles against local German garrisons; attacking rail and road links; ambushing convoys. Before D-Day, the Allied planners argued that little could be expected from the Resistance: the Germans would perceive that its activities across France could be ignored, and concentrate all their resources on the main battle in Normandy. Once Normandy was won, they could deal with the Resistance at leisure; if Normandy was lost, nothing else mattered. This was entirely logical. But it discounted Hitler's obsession with holding territory. He should have abandoned all southern France. Instead, he allowed his Army Group G first to become entangled in irrelevant struggles with the Resistance, and second to be rolled up and destroyed by the American landings in the South of France that began on 15 August. Concentrated around Montauban, 2nd SS Panzer Division should have provided a vital early reinforcement in Normandy. Instead, incredibly, on 7 June it was despatched by road into the Corrèze and Dordogne to suppress local Resistance uprisings. When the order came for the division to entrain for the Channel front, it was a week before it could be disengaged, and the end of June before it could be brought into action.

It is easy to be cynical about the Resistance: so many thousands of recruits rushed to join its ranks in July and August of 1944, having done nothing through the bleak, dangerous years of Occupation; so many vied with each other for the opportunity to execute their fellow-

The French Resistance helped the Allied armies liberate towns in the wake of the retreating Wehrmacht. Here a group of *résistants* escorts a woman accused of being too friendly with the Nazi occupiers.

On 22 August 1944 General Eisenhower gave the order for General Leclerc and the 2nd French Armoured Division to take Paris. Alongside these road signs are American and German unit direction signs, including the name 'Choltitz', the German commander of the Paris garrison.

Spearheaded by the US
79th Infantry Division, the
US XV Corps cross the
River Seine at Mantes-
Gassicourt on 20 August
1944.

countrymen who had collaborated, to torment German prisoners or to shave the heads of women who had been seen too close too often to German soldiers. Yet the Resistance, and above all its uprising after D-Day, contributed immeasurably to the resurrection of the soul of France. Here, at last, amid the great Anglo-American armies rolling across their countryside, Frenchmen could show their contemporaries, and history, that they too had created a legend of Liberation.

As the Allied columns rumbled east through France, they left behind the sullen Norman peasants embittered that their homes and farms had been made a battlefield, and entered towns and villages unscarred by war, where girls hurled flowers at every tank, and euphoric civilians mobbed and cheered each passing unit. At cross-

Vehicles from General Leclerc's 2nd French Armoured Division (or *deuxième division blindé* as they were called) make their dash for Paris on 24 August. *Above* marine gunners drive a captured German *Schwimmwagen*, or amphibious reconnaissance car. *Right* apart from captured equipment, the bulk of the 2nd French Armoured Division was made up of American hardware; here Leclerc's troops are seen in an M3A3 light tank and *far right* in an M4 Sherman tank en route for Paris, with German helmets decorating the front headlights. The insignia of the *deuxième division blindé* can be seen on the side of the tank. On both the *Schwimmwagen* and the M3A3 light tank, red identity panels are prominently displayed to prevent Allied fighter-bombers accidentally shooting at them.

roads and *mairies*, the British and Americans began to meet black-bereted men with rifles slung over their shoulders and the armband of the FFI – *Forces Françaises de l'Intérieur* – above their elbows. In many areas, *résistants* seized civic authority in the wake of the German evacuation and the flight of collaborationist officials. Tricolours, union jacks, stars and stripes suddenly festooned the streets. Although in the cities, and above all in Paris, food had been scarce for years, in the countryside there was still abundance. Calvados, cider, wine, brandy, cheese were pressed upon every truckload of passing men. After the weeks of strain and fear, locked in the hedges of Normandy, there now came the huge exhilaration of release, freedom. Each day the liberators covered as many miles as since D-Day they had fought for yards. Resistance groups fell upon German stragglers pushing for the Seine and beyond, but there was no longer serious organized opposition. Some 300,000 men and 25,000 vehicles from German formations which had escaped the Normandy battle, now

The weapons used by the French Resistance were a mixed bag. Here a French soldier loads a captured German rifle with the enthusiastic assistance of civilians.

retreating from all over western France, were somehow ferried across the great river by engineers in darkness between 20 and 24 August. Hitler cherished delusions that these might form the basis of a new German defensive line along the Somme. But it was too late for all that. Most of the fugitives were directed immediately onwards to the very frontiers of Germany before they paused to regroup, refit, and return to fight again.

It was never the Allies' intention to launch major forces against the city of Paris. They were reluctant to assume the huge liability of feeding its population an hour sooner than was necessary. They were

General Leclerc
(*foreground*) entered Paris
on 25 August. Later that
day General von Choltitz,
commander of the German
garrison (*seated in the
White scout car*)
surrendered to French
troops at the Hôtel
Maurice in the Rue de
Rivoli. This picture shows
their arrival at
Montparnasse Station
together with Colonel Rol-
Tanguy, head of the Paris
Communists (*second from
the left wearing a black
beret*).

Left to right: General von
Choltitz, General Leclerc
and Major-General
Raymond Barton of the US
4th Infantry Division after
the German surrender of
Paris.

General de Gaulle surrounded by French troops after his triumphant entry into Paris.

determined to avoid repeating the great missed opportunity of June in Italy, when lust for glory caused Lieutenant-General Mark Clark to drive headlong for Rome rather than roll up the German forces withdrawing northwards. Throughout the first weeks of August in France, the Allied High Command turned a deaf ear to the pleadings of General Leclerc and his Free French armoured division. Leclerc – his real name was the Vicomte Jacques-Phillipe de Hautecloque, and he had adopted this *nom de guerre* to protect his family in France – was an outstanding soldier who had been with General de Gaulle from the beginning, and brought a column north across the desert from Chad to

This soldier from the *deuxième division blindé* is seen giving an aggressive salute to a German officer.

General de Gaulle with Leclerc and one of his officers from the *deuxième division blindé*.

A senior Wehrmacht officer from the Paris garrison serving as a ceasefire envoy for the *deuxième division blindé* to relay the surrender of the Paris garrison to outlying pockets of German resistance.

join the Anglo-Americans in North Africa. In two weeks of fighting at Alençon and Argentan, he had shown his division to be one of the most vigorous Allied formations in Europe. To Leclerc and his men as they fought east from Normandy, Paris beckoned as the most brilliant jewel of Liberation. In an agony of apprehension and impatience, they awaited news of its fate as the first Americans reached the Seine at Fontainebleau and threw a bridgehead across it.

Amid the national uprising of Resistance after D-Day, in Paris alone de Gaulle had decreed that there should be no insurrection. This was partly to save the city from becoming a battlefield, and partly also because he feared that the Communists – here, as elsewhere, among

A Wehrmacht *Panzerjäger* officer about to set off with a *deuxième division blindé* escort to negotiate the surrender of remaining German resistance. Jeeps flying the white flag of truce were sent out all over Paris.

the most powerful elements of the Resistance – might gain control of the capital. From the beginning, his orders were resented by the Paris FFI and their Communist leader, Colonel Rol-Tanguy. When the Allied breakout from Normandy came at last, their patience snapped. On the afternoon of 17 August, they drew up plans for an uprising to begin the next day, designed to seize control of every major building and key installation in the city. In reality, it quickly became apparent to them that this was too great a task. The uprising was postponed. On 18 August, the National Resistance Council met in the city, and there was a furious argument between Communist and non-Communist resisters about whether they should fight at all. Yet even as the politicians argued, their followers began to act on the streets. Tensions were already acute, with rail and police strikes in effect and the Germans and their acolytes close to panic. On the morning of 19 August, 3,000 police resisters entered the Prefecture, hoisted the tricolour above its roof, and prepared to withstand siege. Bowing to the inevitable, Rol, the FFI's commander, retired to his headquarters

There was still fighting in the streets of Paris after the German surrender and liberation ceremonies were often interrupted by gunfire. Nearly 1,000 members of the FFI died in the fighting. The pictures on this and the following three pages show American and French regular troops with Resistance volunteers in action against German snipers firing from the Paris rooftops.

in the basement of the Paris sewage administration in Montparnasse, and issued orders to all the groups that he could reach that they should take to the streets. By the afternoon of 19 August, his men held many key buildings throughout the city, and intermittent small-arms fire was echoing through the streets. On that first day 50 Germans and 125 Parisians died, most of them *résistants*.

General Dietrich von Choltitz, commander of the German garrison of Greater Paris, was taken entirely unawares by the revolt. Although he held no written directive, it was alleged that Hitler had ordered him to raze the city before he abandoned it. He was undoubtedly under orders to defend Paris to the last, and in five years of war he had gained a reputation for unquestioning obedience to orders. Under pressure from Berlin, he had prepared bridges, power plants, railway stations and scores of buildings for demolition. Yet on the morning of 20 August, urged by the Swedish Consul-General Raoul Nordling, he agreed to a truce between the garrison and the Resistance. He was acutely conscious of the weakness of his own 5,000-strong forces, and

also possessed sufficient aesthetic conscience to perceive a responsibility for one of the great cities of Europe. When the truce broke the next day, Monday the 21st, it was the Resistance and not the Germans who started the fighting. By the 22nd, it was apparent that the insurgents were gaining control. Yet von Choltitz now received a new, ferocious order from Hitler: 'In history the loss of Paris always meant the loss of France. Therefore the Führer repeats his order to hold the defence zone in the advance on the city . . . Within the city every sign of incipient revolt must be countered by the sharpest means . . . The Seine bridges will be prepared for demolition. Paris must not fall into the hands of the enemy except as a field of ruins.' That day, von Choltitz asked to see Raoul Nordling once more. He agreed with the Swede that the only means of saving Paris from destruction and anarchy at the hands of the Resistance factions was by a swift Allied takeover. He offered Nordling passage through his lines to report urgently to the Allies. This was one of the most extraordinary episodes of the Second World War, the unlikeliest of triumphs for civilized reason. Von

Choltitz's perverse Prussian sense of honour demanded only that he should be seen to make a show of resistance before surrendering his command to the liberators.

Dwight Eisenhower now faced one of his first major decisions in France. Delegations from the Paris FFI had already besieged his headquarters with warnings and imprecations; de Gaulle was threatening to take Leclerc's division under his own command and lead it to Paris. In the late afternoon of 22 August, the Supreme Commander agreed that Allied forces should take Paris. The order was transmitted to Bradley, and thence to Leclerc, who came shouting to his operations officer: '*Gribius ... mouvement immediat sur Paris!*' Many of his men, from Algiers and Oran and Chad, had never even seen their capital. They drove with their tanks chalked with the names of towns liberated in the invasion battle – Caen and Cherbourg, Rennes and Lisieux, Bayeux and Tilly. Still 120 miles from the city, all through 23 August they dashed headlong towards the suburbs. At Rambouillet, country residence of France's presidents, they found de

All the sentiments of Paris
are summed up by this van
carrying the French,
British, American and
Soviet flags, together with
a hanging effigy of Hitler.

After four years of
occupation spirits ran high
on the day of liberation.
This Citroën car, flying the
Allied flags, celebrates
General Leclerc's entry
into the city.

Gaulle already arrived, in an agony of impatience. The exuberance of
their reception as they passed through each town had slowed the tank
squadrons. De Gaulle was beset by apprehension that the US 4th
Division might reach Paris before Leclerc. 'Go quickly', he told his
divisional commander. 'We cannot have another Commune.'

The three columns approaching the capital by the Pont de Sèvres,
the Porte d'Italie and the Porte d'Orleans met patchy German
resistance at crossroads and villages. All through a wet and overcast
afternoon, the French stalked anti-tank gun positions and machine-
gunners through the suburban streets. At Fresnes, one Sherman tank
commander died within sight of the church where he had been
married. Early on the evening of 24 August, Leclerc unhappily
concluded that he could not enter the city that night. He halted his
tanks to leaguer. But the Americans were now bitterly impatient of
French sluggishness, as they saw it. They had heard reports of the
celebrations in hamlets along the road. Gerow and Bradley exchanged
sarcastic radio comments about Leclerc's men 'dancing to Paris'.
Impulsively, Leclerc determined to send a reconnaissance column
immediately into the city. A captain of the Chad Infantry, Raymond
Dronne, was given a platoon of infantry and a troop of armour. With

The liberating armies were greeted with smiling faces and cries of '*Merci, merci*', as they progressed through the streets of Paris.

The spoils of war. This GI has been well rewarded for his role in the liberation.

these alone, he set out for Paris.

In the gathering dusk, they drove through the Porte de Gentilly, across the Place d'Italie, and over the Seine by the Pont d'Austerlitz. At 9.30 pm Dronne halted his men outside the Hôtel de Ville, a short walk from von Choltitz's headquarters. The bells were ringing and great crowds gathered across the city. Von Choltitz held up the telephone receiver so that the Chief-of-Staff at Army Group B might hear the sounds. In the early hours of 25 August, Leclerc's armour drove in force into the heart of the city amid passionate scenes of emotion, and sporadic outbreaks of gunfire. At 2.30 that afternoon, von Choltitz surrendered. Nearly a thousand members of the FFI had died in the fighting. Intermittent exchanges with snipers, stragglers,

fugitive collaborators continued through the days that followed. Firing could still be heard on 26 August, when de Gaulle led his officers and a great crowd of *résistants* on a triumphal march from the Arc de Triomphe to Notre Dame for a Te Deum of thanksgiving. On 29 August, a great Allied parade was held in the city, attended by Eisenhower himself, at which the US 28th Division marched down the Champs Elysées before de Gaulle, Leclerc, Bradley and Gerow on the saluting base. Then, while Leclerc's division remained in temporary control of Paris, the 28th hastened onward to take its place in the Allied line racing to complete the liberation of France.

Patton crossed the Meuse on 31 August, and was at Metz on the Moselle the following day. Brussels fell to the British Second Army on

On 29 August 1944 the US 28th Infantry Division marched down the Champs Elysées in a commemorative Victory Parade. They carried on marching through the city to join the Allied advance racing towards eastern France and the Rhine.

US artillery prime movers in the parade accompanied by enthusiastic Parisian youth.

3 September, after a headlong advance of 110 miles in two days. After their unemotional reception in Normandy, the liberators basked in the ecstatic welcome of the people of Brussels and three days of unbridled celebration. On 4 September, 11th Armoured Division reached Antwerp to find the port intact. There were now perhaps 100 surviving German tanks along the entire Western Front, against over 2,000 in the Allied spearheads; 570 Luftwaffe aircraft against the Allies' 14,000. A great wave of euphoria swept through the liberating armies. Victory seemed tantalizingly close. 'Two and a half months of bitter fighting,' declared an Allied intelligence summary from Eisenhower's headquarters, 'have brought the end of the war in Europe within sight, almost within reach. The strength of the German armies in the West has been shattered. Paris belongs to France again, and the Allied armies are streaming towards the frontiers of the Reich.' It was all true. Yet this vision of imminent victory was to prove a mirage. The great hopes with which the Allies began September 1944 were to end in bitter disappointment by the month's end.

Left to right: André le Troquer, a member of de Gaulle's provisional government, General Koenig, Commander-in-Chief of the FFI and governor of Paris, General de Gaulle, Lieutenant-General Bradley, the US Twelfth Army commander, and Lieutenant-General Hodges, US First Army commander.

General Eisenhower, the SHAEF commander, and his deputy Air Chief Marshal Sir Arthur Tedder, salute the grave of the unknown soldier at the Arc de Triomphe.

The Bridge Too Far

The road bridge at Arnhem was blown up shortly after the Germans had recaptured it from the 2nd Battalion Parachute Regiment, which had seized the northern end on 17 September 1944.

ON 1 SEPTEMBER 1944, Eisenhower took over from Montgomery the direct command of the Allied land forces in North-West Europe. The next day, he was obliged to order his First and Third Armies to halt their drive east until their supplies could be replenished, and lines of communication extended. Each army consumed about 400,000 gallons of fuel a day, and the Third's stocks were reduced to a mere 25,000. Patton fumed: 'No one realizes the terrible value of the "unforgiving minute" except me.' To Eisenhower he exploded: 'My men can eat their belts, but my tanks have gotta have gas. If you let me retain my regular allotment of tonnage, Ike, we could push on to the German frontier and rupture that goddam Siegfried Line. I'm willing to stake my reputation on that.' Eisenhower's irritation with the competing demands of his generals surfaced in his reply: 'Careful, George, that reputation of yours hasn't been worth very much.' But after his great dash across France, Patton in his turn could answer triumphantly: 'That reputation is pretty good now.'

Since June 1944, the plight of the Nazi empire had worsened immeasurably. While the Anglo-American forces were destroying Army Group B and rolling forward to the borders of Germany, on the Eastern Front the Russians inflicted a catastrophe of equal magnitude on Hitler's Army Group Centre. The Red Army's summer offensive,

By the winter of 1944, many Germans were placing their last hopes upon Hitler's 'wonder weapons', such as this Messerschmitt Me262, the world's first operational jet interceptor.

Other German 'wonder weapons' included the V1 flying bomb and the V2 missile. This picture shows the pulse duct engine of a V1. In 1944, 8,500 V1s were launched against Britain.

In September 1944 the V2 rockets were launched. This picture shows the sophisticated liquid fuel rocket engine of a V2 outside a slave labour factory in the Hartz mountains.

which began on 22 June 1944, had driven forward 250 miles in three weeks, annihilating twenty-eight German divisions and approaching within fifty miles of the German border in East Prussia before being compelled to halt by lack of supplies. Hitler was now denied access to vast quantities of vital raw materials and manufactured goods from both his eastern and western empires. The loss of the French Atlantic ports almost overnight removed his ability to pursue an effective U-Boat war in the Atlantic. By September, the Red Army had advanced to the Vistula and had overrun Bulgaria and Roumania.

Yet even now, Germany proved capable of producing miracles. In the face of the devastating Allied bomber offensive, the will of the civilian population remained unbroken, perhaps even strengthened. Germany's industries continued to pour forth sufficient tanks, guns and ammunition to sustain and rebuild some portion of her shattered formations. Shortened supply lines eased the Wehrmacht's difficulties, just as those of their opponents were increased by every mile they advanced from the Channel. The misguided American invasion of southern France relieved pressure on the Italian front sufficiently to enable two *Panzergrenadier* divisions to be rushed north to reinforce the sagging line in the west. The Americans committed great forces to the irrelevant task of seizing the isolated Atlantic ports, above all Brest, where repeated setbacks merely strengthened their resolve to prevail, as a matter of national prestige.

A 4.2-inch mortar at the
moment of firing.

American heavy mortar
detachments in action.

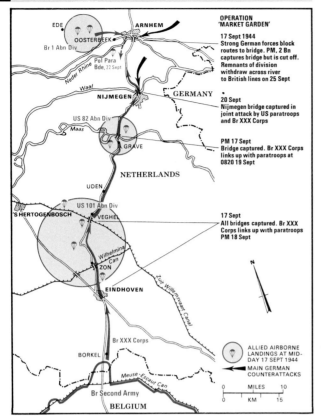

OPERATION 'MARKET GARDEN'

17 Sept 1944
Strong German forces block routes to bridge. PM, 2 Bn captures bridge but is cut off. Remnants of division withdraw across river to British lines on 25 Sept

20 Sept
Nijmegen bridge captured in joint attack by US paratroops and Br XXX Corps

PM 17 Sept
Bridge captured. Br XXX Corps links up with paratroops at 0820 19 Sept

17 Sept
All bridges captured. Br XXX Corps links up with paratroops PM 18 Sept

ALLIED AIRBORNE LANDINGS AT MID-DAY 17 SEPT 1944

MAIN GERMAN COUNTERATTACKS

Operation Market Garden. The advance of XXX Corps was to co-ordinate with the parachute drops, thus achieving maximum surprise.

Field-Marshal Sir Bernard Montgomery, who uncharacteristically gambled with the air drop code-named Operation Market Garden that was designed to seize the bridges across the Rhine.

The British committed an error of omission which proved one of the most costly of the war: in their exhilaration at seizing the port of Antwerp intact, they neglected the importance of hastening onward to seize its north-eastern approaches before these could be put in a state of defence. As was so often the case, the Germans did not make the contrary mistake. They fortified themselves in north-eastern Holland in a fashion that prevented the Allies from making any effective use of Antwerp until the mouth of the Scheldt was cleared in late November. For an army overwhelmingly preoccupied by problems of supply, this was a disaster of the first magnitude.

Since the moment in mid-August when it became apparent that the collapse of Army Group B was imminent, Eisenhower's generals had been locked in a dispute of increasing acrimony about the means by which the campaign was to be carried on after Normandy. Montgomery pressed fiercely for his concept of the 'single thrust', along the northern route through Belgium and Holland, and thence by the shortest route to the Ruhr, the industrial heartland without which Germany could not conceivably continue the war. The German terror-weapon campaign against Britain, with V1 flying bombs and V2 rockets, was also being carried out from launching sites in Holland which the air forces failed to destroy by bombardment. It had become clear that only the Allied occupation of the sites would end the menace which was causing such misery and loss of life in war-weary England.

But while Montgomery's divisions were still crossing the Seine, Patton was approaching the Moselle, and furiously pressing his claims to priority of supply. The manner in which the Germans rushed all their available forces to the Moselle front in the last days of August and first of September made plain their own belief that Patton presented the gravest threat to the West Wall. To Montgomery's bitter and arrogantly expressed fury, Eisenhower compromised. He increased Patton's fuel allocation, while yielding something to Montgomery's aspirations. The Field-Marshal – as he had become since his promotion, to soften the pain of losing the land force command – was compelled to concede that his original concept of 'one really powerful and full-blooded thrust' by forty divisions was implausible. Instead, he now talked of an advance to Berlin – 270 miles distant – by sixteen or eighteen divisions through the Ruhr. Montgomery himself must accept responsibility for one major Allied misfortune at this time: he asked for, and received, the support of the US First Army to secure his right flank. But to achieve this, Hodges' men became helplessly entangled in the fortified zones and industrial jungle around Aachen, where they remained, effectively impotent, for many months to come. The British also suffered severely from a shortage of efficient trucks at this period, when supply lay at the heart of so many problems. Some 1,400 of the British army's vital vehicles were found to be unserviceable with faulty pistons. If this seems a trifling issue, it contributed significantly to the strategic crisis of September.

There is no doubt, also, that in those days, from the summit to the base of the Allied armies, the exhilaration of pursuit caused men fatally to relax. Ultra seemed to confirm for the intelligence staffs the evidence of their own eyes, that the German army in the West was irretrievably broken. 'We shall soon have captured the Ruhr and the Saar and the Frankfurt area,' Eisenhower wrote to Montgomery as late as 15 September, 'and I would like your views as to what we should do next.' A history of 21st Army Group admitted that 'a "war is won" attitude ... prevailed among all ranks.' Against this background of heady optimism, the debate about the future conduct of the campaign seemed much less a matter of life and death than it had done only a few weeks before. The battles for the bridges to the Rhine so often seem to belong to a different age of the war from the struggle for Normandy that it is useful to recall that the landings at Arnhem took place less than a month after Falaise.

History has expressed much wonder that the cautious Montgomery should have been the architect of the extraordinarily bold dash for Arnhem. Yet the grounds for his eagerness become evident, when seen against the background of his struggle with the American generals about the 'single thrust' into Germany. He had lost his case with Eisenhower. Or at least, the Supreme Commander had effectively declined to support any coherent strategy for the defeat of Germany

Over 6,000 British airborne troops were captured after the ill-fated air drop in September 1944. Here a group of survivors are repatriated from a captured German airstrip in 1945.

By 15 December, the Allies were poised for the crossing of the Rhine. But German resistance was strong.

beyond maintaining pressure along the length of the Allied front. But if Operation Market Garden – the 'vertical envelopment' of the bridges to the Rhine – had succeeded, Montgomery would have regained at a stroke the strategic initiative for his offensive on the northern flank. By persuading Eisenhower to attempt this great gamble, Montgomery at once gained the use of the three crack airborne divisions which had been lying idle in England since July, due to a succession of planned parachute drops which were cancelled one by one as victories on the ground overtook their necessity.

The 20,000 men of the US 82nd and 101st Airborne Divisions, together with the British 1st Airborne, landed by parachute and glider along the sixty-mile corridor to the Rhine on 17 September 1944. Their mission was to secure the bridges to the great river, including the last across the Rhine at Arnhem, and hold them for the four days scheduled to allow General Sir Brian Horrocks's British XXX Corps to reach them by road, opening a path into Germany. From the outset, the Americans staged a fine performance. By noon of D+1, the 101st Airborne had seized the bridges at Eindhoven, and the 82nd had gained the bridge over the Maas at Grave. The 82nd crossed the Waal in assault boats under devastating German fire to secure the bridge at Nijmegen. The two American airborne positions then held open the road against intense German pressure while XXX Corps drove on north-eastwards.

The British 1st Airborne, however, was quickly in deep trouble. Its brigades landed between four and ten miles from the bridge at Arnhem to allow them to concentrate after the drop. This was a serious tactical error for lightly-armed airborne troops lacking mobility beyond their own feet, and compelled to fight their way to their objectives. Their arrival on the battlefield was spread over two days, and thereafter supply and reinforcement drops were critically hampered by poor communications. Only one unit, the 2nd Parachute Battalion, moved fast enough through Arnhem to secure the northern end of the bridge. Many other units, going into action for the first time, lacked the essential sense of the urgency of their task. They, like the ground columns, had been briefed to believe that the Germans were at their last gasp. They quickly discovered the extent of their misinformation. Throughout the week of planning before Arnhem, by extraordinary exertions the Germans had everywhere been strengthening their line in the West. Yet the Allies were slow to grasp the new mood and new danger. For years after the war, it was alleged that the planners of Market Garden were unaware of the presence of the 9th SS and 10th SS Panzer Divisions, refitting in the Arnhem area, and now committed to action against 1st Airborne Division with devastating effect. In reality, it is now apparent that the Allied commanders were well aware of the German armoured presence, but declined to allow this to crush all their hopes and ambitions for Market Garden. They knew that most German formations were now mere shells, and indeed the two Panzer divisions amounted only to weak brigade groups in real strength.

But while the Allies' execution of Market Garden was fumbled and in some respects inexcusable – for instance, 1st Airborne's belated discovery on the battlefield that it possessed no effective radio communications, and the poor support afforded to the ground troops by the huge Allied air forces – the Germans responded with their usual ruthless speed and efficiency. Field-Marshal Walther Model chanced to be close at hand when the British landed, and personally directed the operations to frustrate them. The SS crushed 1st Airborne's battalions piecemeal in eight days of bitter fighting, redeemed only by the sacrificial courage of the British paratroopers. German units in the path of XXX Corps' drive for the bridges resisted furiously, assisted by the narrowness of the road, and the impossibility of cross-country movement to outflank the defenders. General Horrocks was a much-loved commander, but it has often been suggested in the years since the battle that his formations did not drive for Arnhem with anything resembling the reckless speed and disregard for casualties that the situation demanded. It is difficult not to contrast the terrible losses endured by the airborne divisions with the mere 130 casualties suffered by Guards Armoured Division, leading XXX Corps between its start line and the bridge at Nijmegen four days later. On Monday 25 September, eight days after the landings, with Colonel John Frost's 2nd Parachute Battalion overwhelmed at Arnhem and only advanced elements of XXX Corps holding a precarious foothold on the opposite

bank of the Rhine, the British faced no choice but that of breaking off the operation and rescuing 2,400 survivors by night evacuation to the south shore. The Germans took more than 6,000 British prisoners. The Allies' last chance of ending the war in 1944 was gone, and the confidence of their commanders had suffered a crushing blow. It remains debatable whether, even if the Arnhem operation had been effective, the British Second Army could have exploited the corridor successfully for a decisive offensive into Germany. The supply problem, the weariness of the Allied troops and the dynamism of the German defenders yet remained to be overcome.

The dash for Arnhem represented the Allies' last spectacular movement of 1944. Thereafter, every yard of ground along the frontiers of the Reich had to be won by costly, dogged fighting amid fierce German counter-attacks, and the worsening European winter weather. This was not a phase of the campaign in which the Allied commanders distinguished themselves. Like their men, they were tired and disappointed by the collapse of so many bright hopes. Along the entire Allied front, attacks were pressed with little imagination or determination. The vigour of local German counter-offensives dismayed men who had believed their enemy to be approaching exhaustion, who enjoyed a numerical superiority of three to one, together with infinite superiority of resources and absolute command of the air. German veterans invariably compared the fighting performance of the Western Allies, and especially of the Americans, unfavourably with

Aachen, the first city in Germany to fall into Allied hands, was taken by the US First Army on 21 October 1944 after fierce fighting.

By the winter of 1944 the
Luftwaffe was reduced to
near impotence. Junkers
JU88s and Messerschmitt
BF110s equipped as night
fighters, seen here at the
end of the war, were
captured on their airfields
where they lay grounded
by lack of fuel.

A Junkers JU87 Stuka, an
obsolete dive bomber
which was used by the
Luftwaffe for attacking
Allied ground targets until
1945.

that of the Russians, though no Anglo-American commander would
have wished to spend lives as prodigally as the Red Army. The supply
problems of the Allies were intensified by their chronic wastefulness:
each American division consumed 720 tons of supplies a day, against
barely 200 for its German counterpart.

Aachen, the first city of Germany to fall into Allied hands, was at
last taken by the US First Army on 21 October after bitter fighting. Yet
beyond the ruins, the victors found that their opponents had created a
formidable new line of defences. Further south, Patton's Third Army
contested the approaches to Metz until 19 November, when they
fought their way into the old fortress town. The same day, the French
5th Armoured Division became the first Allied formation to reach the
Rhine. The French cleared Strasbourg on the 23rd, and held it through
the days that followed against fierce German counter-attacks. On the

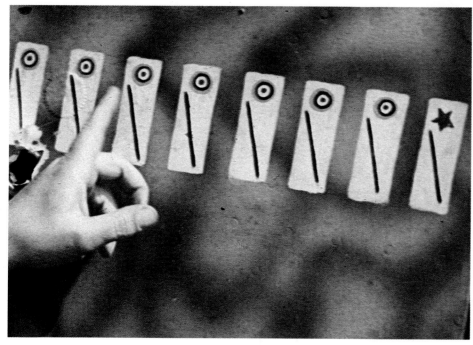

On the tail of this Messerschmitt BF110 night fighter stand the symbols of earlier victories – seven British 'kills' and one Russian.

26th, Bradley's men at last began to claw a path out of the Hürtgen Forest which had delayed them for so long, but by 1 December they had advanced only 1,000 yards beyond it. On 3 December, men of the US 95th Division seized the last intact bridge over the Saar near Saarlautern, and broke into the first bunkers of the Siegfried Line. Model's energetic defensive battles had achieved all that Hitler had wanted: they had won a breathing space for Germany, time to feed more tanks from the factories into the scratch Panzer brigades now facing the great armoured legions of the Allies, time to enable winter to join the struggle alongside the Germans, with low overcast skies thwarting the best efforts of the air forces. Among the Allied armies, no one doubted the inevitability of victory. But waiting for it amid the mud and pine forests of the winter line was a bitter experience for men who yearned so desperately to finish it all, and to go home.

In Germany, Allied bombing was causing extreme shortages of synthetic rubber, medical supplies and fuel. The Luftwaffe had lost its early warning radar in France, while the RAF and USAAF were now able to push forward their own radar guidance stations to the borders of Germany. The Russians were fighting in East Prussia, suffering terrible casualties but also inflicting them. At every stage of the battle on the Eastern Front, the Wehrmacht extracted a huge price from the Red Army for its advances. But this Stalin was willing and able to pay, while Hitler's divisions were being relentlessly reduced without hope of replacement. The health of the Führer himself was visibly failing, his dependence upon drugs, his spasms of exhaustion and depression increasing. One of his officers, departing to take up a front-line command, asked what he should tell the men of his new unit: 'I know what I must not say, but not what I should.' Hitler answered wearily: 'You know for yourself how black things look. Tell them I am thinking and fighting all day and night for the German people and that my thoughts are always out there with my troops. I did try – and I will keep trying – to bring this war to a happy conclusion yet. But you know the way our Luftwaffe is, and there's no point in concealing it.'

Yet the great enigma of this phase of the war was not Hitler's readiness to drag Germany down into catastrophe amid the fall of his empire, but the willingness of his people to endure, and to fight so hard, until the bitter end. The Allies' public commitment to wage war until Germany surrendered unconditionally was undoubtedly a factor. Many, perhaps most, Germans sincerely believed that defeat would signal a new dark age for their country, in which their land would be reduced to a pastoral wilderness and their people to slavery at the hands of the Russians. As an infantry NCO of the Wehrmacht declared: 'If the prospect before me was to chop wood for the remainder of my days in Siberia or Canada, I would prefer to die on the Western front.' There were still a few fanatics who believed that the 'wonder weapons' – V2 rockets, the new generation of U-Boats, the Luftwaffe's jet aircraft – could turn the tide of the war against the Allies. The most objective post-war historian of the SS has written: 'The military significance of the Waffen SS is to be found not so much in its accomplishments during the years of German victory, as in its

A Mitchell B-25 bomber,
converted to a transport
vehicle, taking off.

victories during the years of German defeat.' Even many ordinary
Germans seemed driven by some deep-rooted perception of duty
incomprehensible to their fellow-citizens of Europe. This was the same
instinct which caused many honourable and decent German soldiers
to be shocked by the supposed treachery of the anti-Hitler plotters
who sought to kill him with Count von Stauffenburg's bomb on 20 July
1944. As long as there was a Germany, they were willing to fight in her
army. As long as there was an army, they were willing to serve it in the
fashion which had made them, throughout history, the most formidable soldiers in Europe.

If the Germans entered the winter of 1944 in desperate straits, the
plight of the Allied armies seemed less than happy. 'The war of
attrition in the winter months,' Montgomery wrote, '... was becoming
very expensive in human life. In the American armies there was a
grave shortage of ammunition. The rifle platoons in all divisions were
understrength and the reinforcement situation was bad. American
divisions in the line began to suffer severely from trench-foot as the
winter descended on us.'

But it was the delay in the coming of victory, not any fear of defeat,
that afflicted the Field-Marshal and his American colleagues. On 16
December 1944, he issued an appreciation to his armies: 'The enemy is
at present fighting a defensive campaign on all fronts; his situation is
such that he cannot stage major offensive operations.' Feeling tired
and in need of a break from the frustrating winter routine of his
Tactical Headquarters, he took off in his personal aircraft for
Eindhoven to play a relaxing round of golf.

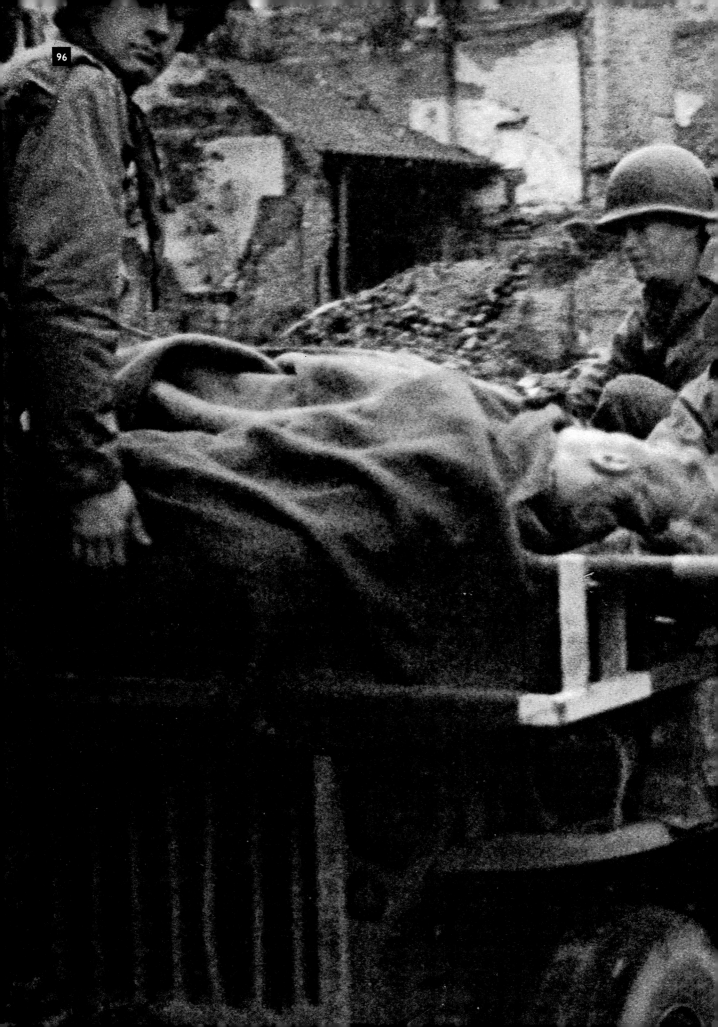

CHAPTER FIVE

The Ardennes Offensive

The American army suffered 81,000 casualties including 19,000 killed in the Battle of the Bulge.

Many towns in the Ardennes were completely destroyed in the fierce fighting, as was the case at St Vith.

ON 16 SEPTEMBER 1944, Adolf Hitler presided over a critical meeting of Germany's generals in the study of his underground headquarters in East Prussia, the 'Wolf's Lair'. As General Alfred Jodl, chief of OKW's Operations Staff, was describing his fears that the advancing Americans might break into Germany through the woods and hills of the Ardennes, where only negligible German forces stood in their path, Hitler suddenly interrupted him.

'I have made a momentous decision', he declared fervently. 'I shall go over to the offensive, that is to say' – he slapped the map on the desk before him – 'here, out of the Ardennes, with the objective, Antwerp!' Exactly three months later, at 5.30 am on an icy, foggy morning along a sixty-mile front reaching down the borders of Luxembourg and Belgium, his armies launched their last great attack of the war exactly as Hitler had planned, hitting four weak American infantry divisions with twenty German, seven of these Panzer, and mustering almost a thousand tanks and assault guns.

The Ardennes offensive has chiefly fascinated history because it

The quiet before the storm: in mid-December, the Americans settled down in the Ardennes, expecting their slow advance into Germany to continue. Hitler had other plans.

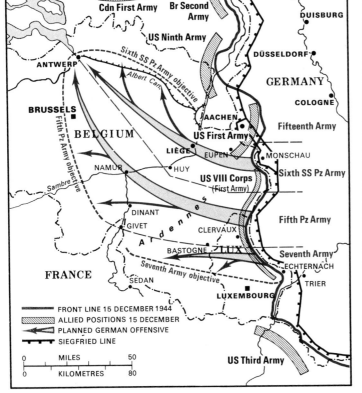

Hitler's plan was to break through the Allied front in the Ardennes, separate the British and American troops and capture Antwerp.

achieved absolute surprise. How was it possible, with all the vast intelligence and air reconnaissance resources of the Allies, above all Ultra, that Hitler could still inflict upon them the greatest shock of the campaign in North-West Europe? In the weeks before Operation *Wacht Am Rhein* was launched, the Allies had ample notice of the withdrawal of the Panzer divisions from the German front for refitting. There was much speculation among intelligence officers as to whether the intention was merely to create a Panzer reserve in readiness to meet the next major Allied offensive, or whether some greater purpose was afoot. The overwhelming consensus was that the Germans neither intended, nor were capable of, anything more than a spoiling attack in advance of the next Allied thrust. In the first week of December General Kenneth Strong, Eisenhower's Chief-of-Intelligence, voiced his suspicion that the Americans might be in for 'a nasty little Kasserine' – a reference to the Germans' crushing surprise offensive in North Africa in 1943. Bradley told General Courtney Hodges, commanding the US First Army, that if the Germans were to

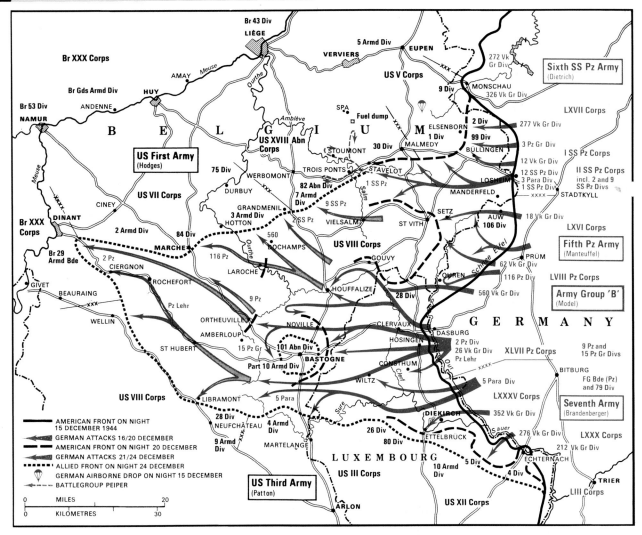

The Germans' daring assault nearly succeeded. But with empty fuel tanks and increasing opposition from Allied troops, the Ardennes offensive ground to a halt.

attack on the weakly defended Ardennes front, his men would stage a fighting retreat as far as the Meuse, if necessary. He also warned Middleton, commanding the US VIII Corps in the Ardennes, not to hold major fuel or supply dumps in the threatened forward area. But none of these officers took each others' remarks very seriously. Nor did First Army make much of the inspired hunch of its intelligence chief, Colonel Benjamin Dickson, that an Ardennes offensive was imminent. That officer's credibility had been low since the night he burst into the First Army commander's sleeping caravan to report German radio intercepts that von Rundstedt was calling on the Wehrmacht to throw down its arms and abandon the war. It was then found that he had been listening, in reality, to an American 'black propaganda' transmission.

But the root reason for the Allies' failure to read the signs from the snowladen forests beyond their front was that all military logic, even sanity, argued against a major German offensive. Von Rundstedt, commanding Hitler's armies in the West, was a conservative officer who conducted his defensive battles 'by the book'. For a commander whose resources were strained to the limits in containing successive Allied offensives, it would have been an act of madness to squander men and resources in an attack which could end in only one fashion, given the Allies' massive strategic superiority.

What the Allied commanders could not have known was that Hitler

had forced his winter offensive upon his commanders despite their bitter opposition. Even Sepp Dietrich, the Führer's old bodyguard who now commanded Sixth Panzer Army because of Hitler's absolute faith in his loyalty, was shocked by the plan: 'All Hitler wants me to do is to cross a river, capture Brussels, and then go on and take Antwerp! And all this in the worst time of the year through the Ardennes where the snow is waist deep and there isn't room to deploy four tanks abreast let alone armoured divisions! Where it doesn't get light until eight and it's dark again at four and with reformed divisions made up chiefly of kids and sick old men – and at Christmas!' The corps and divisional commanders responsible for the assault were briefed personally by their Führer at an extraordinary meeting at von Rundstedt's headquarters in Ziegenberg Castle. In the shadow of the July bomb plot, every general was relieved of his sidearm and briefcase before being permitted to sit down, and an armed SS guard stood behind each chair. Fritz Bayerlein of *Panzer Lehr* said that he was afraid to reach for his handkerchief. The generals were shocked by the spectacle of the broken man who addressed them, delivering a two-hour harangue that encompassed Frederick the Great, the destiny of his people, the need now to demonstrate the absolute resolve of Germany. Not one of his senior officers believed in the feasibility of what they were being asked to do. Hitler declined their proposals for a

An armed Belgian civilian and a member of the US military police on checkpoint duty. Reports of German troops disguised as American soldiers for sabotage missions led to the introduction of massive security checks during the German offensive.

much more limited operation, designed merely to envelop the American forces around Aachen. He also refused to acknowledge the critical importance of the lack of fuel for the Panzer divisions, which were to attack with a bare minimum of petrol reserves.

Just before 5.30 am on 16 December 1944, American soldiers, huddled in their frozen outposts along the Our river, telephoned their command post to report curious flickering pinpoints of light deep in the German lines. Seconds later, as a deluge of shellfire began to land in their midst, they understood the significance of the vision. The dim shapes of German infantry began to swirl out of the fog masking much of the front that morning, catching Americans in their chow lines and blankets and at their fatigues, bringing chaos to a command structure

Christmas fell rather inconveniently in the middle of the battle. Here two GIs decorate a Christmas tree set up in the street.

bereft of telephone lines due to shellfire and sabotage, confused by the poor visibility, and utterly unprepared. The first tanks of Dietrich's Sixth Panzer Army attacked between Monschau and Losheim on the German right, with General Hasso von Manteuffel's Fifth Panzer Army in the centre, and General Brandenberger's infantry of Seventh Army securing the southern flank of the armoured advance. They were 100 miles from Antwerp, attacking through some of the wildest terrain in western Europe, a region devoid of railways or cities or major roads. The Allies had rejected the Ardennes out of hand as a suitable route into Germany. Yet the Germans had already achieved the impossible once by this path, in 1940. Could they not achieve the miracle a second time?

Hand grenades assume the unusual function of Christmas tree decorations.

A Belgian boy, probably homeless due to the fighting in the Ardennes, seems to have been adopted as a mascot by the GIs.

A Belgian girl shows her happiness after receiving a Christmas present from a GI Santa Claus.

The northern axis of the assault quickly suffered a serious check as a result of a fine American stand at Monschau. The German infantry divisions had been made up to strength with large numbers of undertrained and inadequate replacements, and exhibited incomparably less skill and determination than the SS Panzer divisions. The American defenders killed them in large numbers in the first days of the assault. Elsewhere along the front, German tanks poured through the defences. But their advance was slowed by pockets of fierce American resistance, and by the difficulties of moving armour forward in close country amid steep ravines and river obstacles. Within hours, the offensive had fallen behind schedule. The Germans always knew that to have a remote hope of success, speed was vital. Already their commanders were gloomy. The shoulders of the Allied line were holding. There were as yet no broken Allied banks where the 'expanding torrent' of the Panzers could widen their breach.

Yet on that first day, the Allied response was slow. Poor communications caused news of the scale of the attack to seep back slowly to the High Command. Bradley was at first loathe to transfer armoured divisions to the threatened front because of the delays this would impose upon Third Army's scheduled offensive further south. Only on Eisenhower's insistence was the order finally given. Even Hodges at First Army, in the path of the onslaught, was unwilling to cancel his imminent attack on the Roer Dams, believing the German operation to be a mere spoiling movement. The Allied commanders were reluctant to acknowledge that their intelligence could have been so disastrously wrong. Only on the next day, the 17th, as everywhere along the Ardennes front German armour began to roll forward through the

No place to hide: civilians flee the advancing Germans, fearful of a new Nazi occupation.

crumbling American defences, did they grasp the seriousness of the crisis. An Ultra intercept reached Eisenhower and Bradley: 'Rundstedt on sixteenth informed soldiers of West Front that hour of destiny had struck. Mighty offensive armies face Allies. Everything at stake. More than mortal deeds for Fatherland and Führer. A quote holy duty unquote.' On the night of the 16th, Hitler telephoned the commander of Army Group G on the front south of the Ardennes: 'Balck! Balck!' he proclaimed. 'Everything has changed in the West! Success – complete success – is now in our grasp!'

After the initial sluggishness of the Allied response, in the days following the 16th, their mood swung dramatically to near panic. Reports of the activities of Colonel Otto Skorzeny's commandos, attacking communications behind the lines in American uniforms, caused alarm throughout the battle areas far out of proportion to the material damage Skorzeny's men achieved. Eisenhower and his

A civilian picks through the wreckage of his home in Bastogne.

commanders were under heavy guard throughout the following week, and movement among the armies was hampered by incessant security checks by nervous soldiers. 'Where the hell has this sonofabitch gotten all his strength?' Bradley demanded in bewilderment as he studied intelligence reports of the German battle order deployed for the offensive. By the morning of the 18th, Hodges learned that elements of Sixth Panzer Army had crossed the Amblève river, passed through Stavelot and were approaching his own headquarters at Spa, which were hastily moved. *Kampfgruppe Peiper*, commanded by the 29-year-old SS Colonel Joachim Peiper, one of the most formidable tank officers of the war, faced an almost open road to a vast, vital American fuel dump holding two and a half million gallons of petrol. Yet here, in a narrow defile thirty miles from their start line, General Dietrich's armour was checked by American reinforcements and a barrier of blazing fuel, created on their own initiative by men of the first Belgian unit to be formed after their liberation. Peiper's probes to find alternative lines of advance were repelled, above all by the courage and determination of American engineer detachments blowing bridges in his path. He found himself isolated, miles ahead of Dietrich's other divisions. His attack fizzled out. The exhausted SS officer is said to have sat on his turret pounding one knee with his fist in sheer frustration, repeating again and again: 'The damned engineers! The damned engineers!' A German parachute drop intended to block Allied reinforcements from the north had been executed in chaos, to the fury of its commander, Colonel Friedrich von der Heydte, who jumped himself with one arm in a splint from an earlier injury. Von der Heydte's scattered survivors could only harass American positions in their area.

The American 82nd and 101st Airborne Divisions moved forward to take over the defence of key road junctions amid massive traffic jams caused by the stream of support troops, rear units, stragglers and fugitives blocking roads away from the front. Many of the paratroops had been mobilized at such short notice that they moved forward without weapons, helmets or winter clothing. But these, the outstanding fighting infantry of the US Army, reached the battlefield at a critical moment. American emotions about the situation were heightened by news of the killing of some ninety prisoners of war by men of the SS at Malmédy on the 17th. Although it would be foolish to deny that, in the course of the campaign in North-West Europe, all the combatant armies shot prisoners on occasions, in the Ardennes, the SS divisions behaved with exceptional ruthlessness and indifference to humanity. Both sides recognized that they were engaged in a mortal struggle.

Von Manteuffel's Fifth Panzer Army made better progress than Dietrich's divisions in the first stage of the offensive. On Manteuffel's front, the Germans met the American 106th Division, fresh to battle, underarmed, underled, and psychologically entirely unprepared for the onslaught that faced them in a sector where they were alleged to be receiving a gentle introduction to war. After resisting effectively at some points on the 16th, the next day two of the encircled regiments of the 106th surrendered, the Panzers seizing more than 7,000 prisoners. The 106th Division's commander, General Alan Jones, seemed to become paralyzed by the disaster that struck his command. The

American official historians later described this defeat on the Schnee Eifel as 'the most serious reverse suffered by American arms during the operations of 1944–45 in the European theatre.' The US 28th Division, sent to an outpost line near the River Our to recover from heavy fighting and heavy losses, checked the Germans on the first day but could not halt them. Everywhere, in their foxholes and bunkers amidst the pine trees and the snow, the defenders faced an unequal struggle, meeting Tiger and Panther tanks without their own armoured support and with only inadequate anti-tank guns. What was remarkable about the fighting of those first days in the Ardennes was not that some American units collapsed, but that so many stood and fought to such effect. On 18 December, thirty miles deep in the American front, Fifth Panzer Army approached the key road junction at Bastogne. The following morning, the Germans attempted to storm the American positions. But here, at a turning point of the battle, they were repulsed. A bitter battle began which continued throughout the week that followed. Manteuffel was determined to bypass Bastogne, but met new American formations now being pushed into the line in

The family portraits still hang on the wall of a wrecked home.

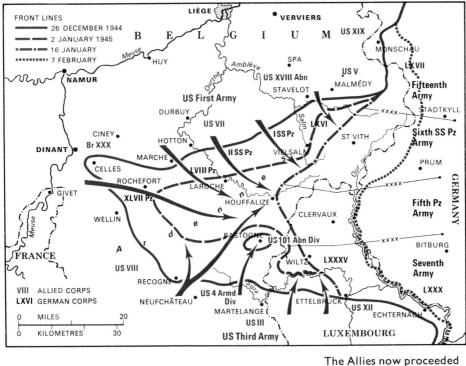

The Allies now proceeded to crush the German 'bulge'. The battle for Bastogne was the scene of some of the bitterest fighting of the war.

great strength. Two of Patton's corps from Third Army wheeled northward to relieve Bastogne, and began to fight their way up the road to the town. Manteuffel was compelled to divert his flagging formations to resist the American attacks, rather than to press on for the Meuse. Only a single isolated German unit reached to within four miles of the river at Dinant. This was rapidly crushed by the Allies. The fuel shortage caused critical difficulties in bringing forward German artillery, much of which never came within range of the Allied lines. On 23 December, after a week in which fog rendered the Allied forces impotent, the skies cleared. The huge weight of air power began to fall upon the Germans with terrible effect. The efforts of the Luftwaffe to support the offensive merely sufficed to add a long roll call of lost German aircraft to the price of battle.

The defence of Bastogne against 2nd Panzer, *Panzer Lehr* and the 26th *Volksgrenadier* Division from 20 to 26 December became an epic of the American army, redeeming all the misfortunes of its shattered formations in the first days of the battle. The 101st Airborne Division commanded by Brigadier-General Anthony G. McAuliffe, supported by tanks of the 9th Armoured and two battalions of engineers, held out among the battered ruins of the town against repeated German assaults. A demand from the Germans to surrender on the 22nd was met with McAuliffe's legendary rejoinder 'Nuts!' The following day, air supply drops and fighter-bomber support improved the position

The three German armies engaged in the Ardennes offensive entered the battle half-a-million-men strong and suffered over 100,000 casualties. These prisoners were the lucky ones.

along the sixteen-mile American perimeter. An all-out German attack on Christmas Day merely cost Manteuffel's divisions heavy tank casualties. At 4.45 pm the following afternoon, tanks of Patton's 4th Armoured Division reached Bastogne and raised the siege, after fighting a series of bitter battles on the road northwards against the German 5th Parachute Division.

While Patton directed operations against the southern flank of the German salient, Montgomery assumed command of the north, including the US First and Ninth Armies, given to him by Eisenhower. The outstanding Collins of the US VII Corps took direct battlefield control of the counter-attack from the north. On 26 December, the Germans at last acknowledged that they could not advance further westwards. '*Mein Führer*,' Jodl told Hitler baldly, 'we must face the facts squarely and openly. We cannot force the Meuse river.' Hitler would not agree: 'We have had unexpected setbacks,' he said, 'because my plan was not followed to the letter.' Yet even if the Germans had reached the Meuse in strength, it is unlikely that they could have progressed beyond it. Many of the reserves ordered by Hitler to join the offensive never even reached the forward areas, held back either by chronic traffic jams in the narrow corridors forward, or lacking petrol to move. Hitler insisted that the struggle for Bastogne must continue, but events had long since overtaken him. The German spearhead units began to fall back all along their front. Many tanks, drained of fuel, were

A knocked-out German assault gun or *Sturmgeschütz*. The ripple finish, known as *zimmerit* and made of resin, was designed to prevent magnetic bombs adhering to the surface. The German Panzer divisions taking part in the Ardennes offensive suffered heavy losses, including 800 irreplaceable tanks.

For the first week of the offensive fog grounded the Allied airforces. On 23 December 1944, the skies cleared. This picture shows the vapour trails made by Allied aircraft on their way to attack German supply lines and armoured columns in the Ardennes.

abandoned. The survivors of Peiper's battlegroup were compelled to escape on foot.

Some 600,000 Americans were committed to the Battle of the Bulge, as it became known, before its conclusion. They suffered 81,000 casualties, including 15,000 captured and 19,000 killed. The British, who only entered the battle in its closing phase, lost 1,400. The Germans employed almost half a million men, and lost at least 100,000 of them. Each side lost around 800 tanks. Those of the Allies were replaced within a matter of days. The German Panzer divisions could never be substantially rebuilt, and the Luftwaffe had lost hundreds of irreplaceable aircraft. For the Germans, the Ardennes offensive ended in utter failure, with huge losses of men and *matériel* for no worthwhile gain, exactly as von Rundstedt and his colleagues had anticipated. The Allies had suffered a traumatic shock, which they afterwards believed had set back their battle for Germany by six weeks. Anglo-American relations suffered a further blow with the conduct of Montgomery after he was placed in command of the northern flank. He arrived at Hodges' headquarters, in the words of a staff officer, 'like Christ come to cleanse the temple.' His behaviour to Bradley on Christmas Day, when they met at Zonhoven, surpassed reason. He lectured the American general about the reasons for his armies' misfortune: 'I said the Germans had given us a real "bloody nose"; it was a proper defeat, and we had much better admit it.' Montgomery declared that the situation was entirely the consequence of Eisenhower's failure to pursue the 'single thrust' strategy into Germany under his own command. Yet now, the Field-Marshal showed no interest in mounting a major counter-attack against the reeling Germans, and declared his opinion that Hodges' army would be unfit to resume the offensive for months.

If Montgomery's cool efficiency was useful during the course of the battle, not least in securing the Meuse against a possible German breakthrough, he must bear a large share of responsibility for the Allied failure to turn on the Germans when their offensive lost momentum. Despite the passionate impatience of Collins, Montgomery refused to allow VII Corps to begin its offensive alongside the British until 3 January. Throughout the last days of 1944, while the Americans correctly judged that the German effort was spent, the British 21st Army Group continued to assert its fears that the enemy still possessed the energy for one more thrust. Beyond this there was also Montgomery's undoubted low opinion of the capabilities of the American armies. His outrageous declaration to the world after the battle that the British had saved the Americans from imminent collapse caused deep bitterness between the Allies. The Ardennes campaign was, from beginning to end, an American battle and an American triumph. During the struggle from the beaches of Normandy, there had been moments for doubting the quality of the American soldier. Hitler described the Americans contemptuously as 'the Allies' Italians'. But in the battle for the Ardennes, against the finest troops Germany could still put into the field, the US army showed a new skill and maturity as a fighting force.

In the first weeks of 1945, having halted the Germans, the Allies mounted an offensive to drive them from the 'bulge' that they had won at such cost. Characteristically, the enemy fought a series of dogged, stubborn, defensive battles for every town and village before it was yielded. Amid ice and snow that hampered the advance of the armoured columns and made life in the front line unforgivingly bitter for the men of the opposing armies, the Americans retook St Vith on 23 January, a month after its loss, and crossed the Our and the Clerf rivers. As the Allied commanders paused to take stock, they were dismayed by the number of Germans and the quantity of equipment that had been allowed to escape from the salient. After the Panzers' shattering repulse in the last week of December, with imaginative leadership and ruthless will, it should have been possible to cut the base of the German bulge and ensure that both Dietrich's and Manteuffel's formations never escaped east to rejoin the defence of the Reich. 'If you get a monkey in the jungle hanging by his tail,' said Patton, 'it is easier to get him by cutting his tail than kicking him in the face.' Instead, once again, ponderous Allied movement denied the Americans and the British the all-embracing victory that should have been theirs. Churchill called the Ardennes 'the greatest American battle of the war'. It was the Allies' misfortune that they did not reap the full fruits of their success, which might have enabled them to complete the destruction of the German army in the west many weeks, and many lives, before May 1945.

For these two Germans the war ended in December 1944.

The Road to the Elbe

The first units of Marshal
Koniev's 1st Ukrainian
Front to reach the River
Elbe were from 58th
Guards Rifle Division, in
which this young
bemedalled soldier served.

EVERY GREAT Russian offensive of the war was followed by a lull while the Red Army reorganized its over-stretched supply lines, and gathered its strength for the next phase of the battle. The pause in major Russian activity after the summer campaign of 1944 was exceptionally protracted. It continued into the new year of 1945, incurring the Western Allies' bitter criticism and suspicion when Stalin's divisions failed to march into Warsaw and relieve the partisans, whose uprising was finally crushed on 2 October, after the loss of a quarter of a million Polish lives. The Allies believed that the Russians wanted the non-Communist Polish resistance shattered for political reasons of their own. As months dragged on without renewed Russian activity, all the old British and American doubts were reborn as to what their Eastern ally could do. Was the Red Army at last exhausted? Had the Germans fought it to a standstill on the Vistula line? Were its commanders capable of orchestrating a great new attack appropriate to the massed millions of armed men they had now assembled between the Baltic Sea and the Carpathians?

The crisis in the Ardennes thrust aside all these doubts. The Western Allies now cared only that Stalin should act urgently to relieve the pressure in the West. The Russian new year offensive was

Although they look friendly enough here, the soldiers of the Red Army, whose country had lost 20 million dead in four years of war, inflicted a terrible revenge upon the German people.

scheduled for 20 January. Could it be mounted sooner? Churchill cabled Stalin: 'The battle in the West is very heavy. I regard the matter as urgent.' Tedder, Eisenhower's deputy, was dispatched to Moscow to plead the case for haste. Stalin acceded, though by the time his men had moved the crisis in the West was over. On 12 January 1945, Marshal I.S. Koniev's armies were launched from the Baranów bridgehead, seventy divisions strong supported by two air armies. At first, the same winter fog that had hung low over the Ardennes for so much of the western battle impeded Soviet air power and confused the assaulting troops. But on the third day the attack broke through to Pińczów, and Russian armour began to pour through the gap. On the 14th also, Marshal G. Zhukov launched his own offensive further north, wheeling around Warsaw which fell on the 17th. On the 19th, Koniev's men reached the borders of Silesia, the industrial region of Germany second only to the Ruhr in importance. By the end of its first week, the offensive was 100 miles forward from its start line, on a front of almost 400 miles.

Hitler, characteristically, transformed defeat into disaster. His newly-appointed Chief-of-Staff, General Heinz Guderian, pleaded in vain to be allowed to evacuate by sea the army group of twenty-six

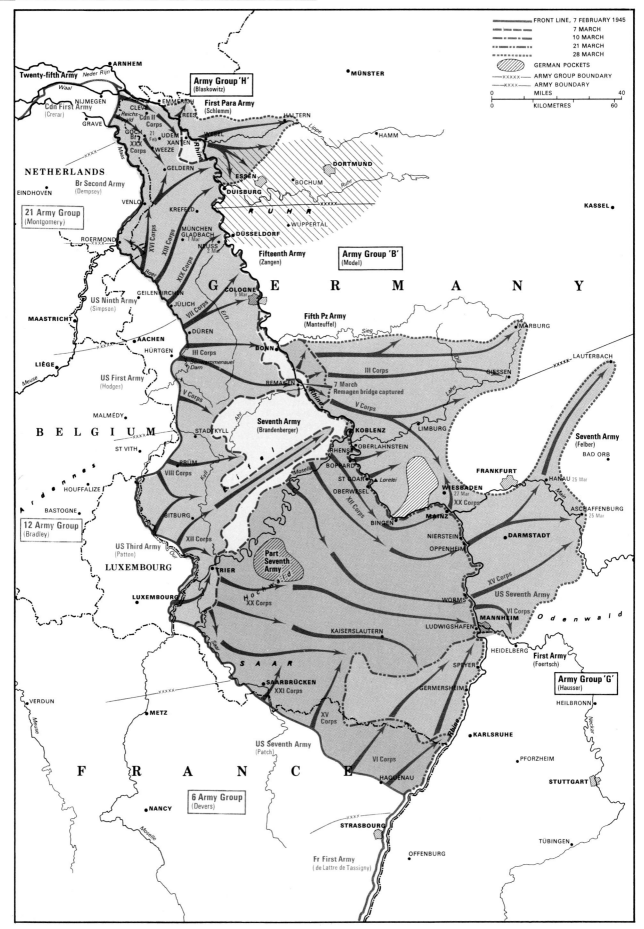

FRONT LINE, 7 FEBRUARY 1945
7 MARCH
10 MARCH
21 MARCH
28 MARCH
GERMAN POCKETS
XXXXX — ARMY GROUP BOUNDARY
XXXX — ARMY BOUNDARY
MILES
0 · · · · · · · · 40
KILOMETRES
0 · · · · · · · · · 60

ARNHEM
Neder Rijn
Twenty-fifth Army
Waal
NIJMEGEN
Cdn First Army
(Crerar)
GRAVE
Reichs-
wald
Cdn II
Corps
CLEVE
EMMERICH
REES
GOCH
Br 7
XXX
Corps
21
Feb
UDEM
XANTEN
WEEZE
Army Group 'H'
(Blaskowitz)
First Para Army
(Schlemm)
HALTERN
WESEL
Lippe
HAMM
MÜNSTER

NETHERLANDS
Br Second Army
(Dempsey)
GELDERN
ESSEN
DUISBURG
DORTMUND
BOCHUM
Ruhr
KASSEL

EINDHOVEN
VENLO
KREFELD
MÜNCHEN
GLADBACH
1 Mar
NEUSS
2 Mar
R U H R
WUPPERTAL
DÜSSELDORF

21 Army Group
(Montgomery)
ROERMOND
Roer
XVI Corps
XIII Corps
XIX Corps
Fifteenth Army
(Zangen)
Army Group 'B'
(Model)

US Ninth Army
(Simpson)
GEILENKIRCHEN
JÜLICH
G E R M A N Y
COLOGNE
5 Mar
Erft
VII Corps
Fifth Pz Army
(Manteuffel)
MARBURG
Sieg

MAASTRICHT
AACHEN
DÜREN
III Corps
BONN
III Corps
Lahn
GIESSEN
LAUTERBACH
XXXXX

LIÈGE
HÜRTGEN
Schwammenauel
Dam
REMAGEN
7 March
Remagen bridge captured
Rhine
V Corps
LIMBURG

US First Army
(Hodges)
V Corps
Meuse
MALMÉDY
STADTKYLL
Seventh Army
(Brandenberger)
KOBLENZ
OBERLAHNSTEIN
Seventh Army
(Felber)
BAD ORB

B E L G I U M
ST VITH
XXXX
PRÜM
Kyll
RHENS
BOPPARD
Moselle
ST GOAR
Lorelei
FRANKFURT
HANAU 25 Mar
ASCHAFFENBURG
25 Mar

A r d e n n e s
HOUFFALIZE
BASTOGNE
VIII Corps
OBERWESEL
XII Corps
BINGEN
WIESBADEN
27 Mar
XX Corps
MAINZ

12 Army Group
(Bradley)
BITBURG
XII Corps
Part
Seventh
Army
NIERSTEIN
OPPENHEIM
DARMSTADT

US Third Army
(Patton)
LUXEMBOURG
Our
TRIER
Hochwald
XX Corps
WORMS
XV Corps
US Seventh Army
VI Corps
MANNHEIM
Odenwald

LUXEMBOURG
Saar
KAISERSLAUTERN
LUDWIGSHAFEN
HEIDELBERG
First Army
(Foertsch)

S A A R
SAARBRÜCKEN
XXI Corps
SPEYER
Army Group 'G'
(Hausser)
HEILBRONN

VERDUN
XXXXX
METZ
XV
Corps
GERMERSHEIM
Rhine
KARLSRUHE

Meuse
Saar
US Seventh Army
(Patch)
VI Corps
HAGUENAU
PFORZHEIM

F R A N C E
NANCY
6 Army Group
(Devers)
Moselle
XXXX
STRASBOURG
OFFENBURG
Neckar
STUTTGART
TÜBINGEN

Fr First Army
(de Lattre de Tassigny)

Field-Marshal
Montgomery's crossing of
the Rhine on 23 March 1945
was accompanied by
massive 'carpet bombing'.

Left by the end of March
1945 the Allies had cleared
the Rhine from Nijmegen
to Mannheim.

divisions isolated in the Baltic states. His leader insisted that they must continue to defend the U-Boat development and testing areas which were vital to his plans for the new campaign at sea. During Guderian's absence from his headquarters just before the Russian offensive, Hitler seized the opportunity to dispatch two Panzer divisions south from Poland into Hungary for an attempt to relieve Budapest. After driving twenty-five miles towards the beleaguered garrison, the attack collapsed in costly failure. On the Vistula line itself, Hitler rejected all pleas that the German defenders should be permitted to 'roll with the punch', and fall back before the Russian onslaught. Instead, they were compelled to stand and die where they stood. They inflicted huge casualties on the Russians before they were overrun. But Germany's strength in the east had been critically eroded. The Russians took over 100,000 prisoners in the first fortnight of their offensive. After five years in which Europe had seen its peoples of almost every nationality fleeing by the thousand with their pathetic possessions before the Nazi war machine, now for the first time it was

Roll call for GIs of the US 17th Airborne Division, attached to Montgomery's 21st Army Group for airborne operations coinciding with the main assault crossing of the Rhine on 24 March 1945.

the turn of Germans to become refugees. Long columns of hollow-eyed, destitute civilians from the border towns of the east began to trudge westwards, away from the Russians. They knew, as most men of the Wehrmacht knew, that after the terrible sufferings Germany had inflicted upon Russia, with twenty million of her people dead, Stalin's peasant armies would extract a terrible revenge. AJP Taylor has succinctly portrayed Stalin's armies advancing westwards:

'The Soviet army was of a kind never seen in modern warfare. At the head came élite forces, often honoured with the name of Guards divisions: tanks, artillery, rockets, men of high professional competence and technique. Once a breakthrough had been achieved, the inexhaustible mass of infantry followed like a barbarian horde on the march: ill-trained, often undisciplined, and living off the country. Crusts of bread and raw vegetables were their only food... These Russians slaughtered the German infantry, pillaged the towns and villages through which they passed, and raped the women. They were true cannon fodder. After the infantry came another élite corps: the military police, who restored order, shot the worst offenders out of hand, and drove the infantry forward to fresh assaults.'

Eisenhower, at an encounter after the war, described to Zhukov the

Tension shows on the faces of the soldiers as they await their orders to board their gliders.

A GI of the US 17th
Airborne Division
preparing to board.

Ready!

A CG-4 Hadrian troop-
carrying glider being towed
by a C-47 Dakota.

A close-up view of the glider as it becomes airborne.

ingenious technology deployed by the Allies for clearing minefields. The Russian remarked amiably that he had always found that the most efficient means of dealing with minefields was to march infantry through them. The Russians possessed better tanks than the Germans as well as far more of them, and used their massed artillery to formidable effect. Until the very end of the war, the Wehrmacht showed itself more tactically skilful than the Red Army. But in battle after battle, the Germans destroyed wave upon wave of Russian attackers only to find that there was always one more.

On 26 January, in the Russians' northern sector, Marshal K. Rokossovsky's men reached the Gulf of Danzig near Elbing. Koniev crossed the Oder on a 60-mile front, 180 miles from his start line. He thence pushed forward to the River Neisse. By the last days of February 1945, the Russian attack had reached the limits of its strength and supplies, and the defence stabilized. To the Germans'

advantage, their front had now shrunk to less than 200 miles between the Baltic and the Bohemian mountains. Even with their diminished forces, here they could once more create a semblance of a line of resistance. But the Russians were within 60 miles of Berlin. To stem their advance, Hitler had taken the momentous decision to transfer every available reinforcement, every tank and gun emerging from the factories to the east, leaving the Western Front to fend for itself. Thus, when the Western Allies began to move once more, the Germans in their path had no further resources to call up.

In February 1945, to the bitter resentment of the American generals, Eisenhower decreed that the Anglo-Canadian 21st Army Group should mount the major effort of the new offensive, with the US Ninth Army under his command. Though Montgomery would never concede this, until the end of the war Eisenhower gave his northern flank much of the priority that the Field-Marshal had so insistently demanded. The Americans now overwhelmingly dominated the campaign, with forty-seven divisions on the Western Front alongside nineteen shrinking British and Canadian formations. The British were at the limits of their manpower. American vehicles provided much of their transport – and that of the Russians, whose newfound mobility was chiefly based

The pictures on these four pages show some of the colourfully-named gliders taking part in this operation, and on page 131, a GI of the US 17th Airborne Division fully equipped for the landing.

upon thousands of General Motors trucks. American aircraft dominated the skies. American tanks equipped almost all the Western armoured divisions. It was a tribute to Eisenhower's unwearying willingness to compromise for the sake of the Alliance – however unsophisticated his strategic thinking might be – that he granted the British pride of place in this last great Allied push of the war. Indeed, the Rhine crossing was much delayed to allow Montgomery time to prepare his battle in the painstaking fashion he favoured. After the misfortunes wrought by Allied euphoria in September and over-confidence in December, their commanders were now extraordinarily over-cautious, planning a campaign to finish the German war that might last until November.

The American generals' anger and impatience with Montgomery spurred them to exceptional efforts in their own sectors. On 7 March, Patton's tanks broke through the weak German defences in the Eifel. Sixth Panzer Army was gone from the front. Even with the difficulties of snow drifts and rugged terrain, the Americans swarmed through the fabled West Wall. For the first time, the cohesion and determination of the defenders was seen to be flagging. Each day, advancing Americans met groups of Germans walking hesitantly forward beneath a white

flag, arms upraised, even before serious fighting developed. Lieutenant-General William Simpson's Ninth Army crossed the Roer on 23 February. Patton's Third reached the Rhine close to Koblenz after driving sixty miles in three days. The bridges in their path had been destroyed, but further north on 7 March, advanced elements of First Army pushed on to the river at Remagen, near Bonn, and seized the bridge intact by a superbly dashing *coup de main* before the German engineers could blow it. Within hours, American reserves had been rushed forward to secure a bridgehead on the eastern bank. The Americans' impatience with their Allies was redoubled when Eisenhower prohibited any development of the Remagen bridgehead because it ran contrary to established plans. 'What in hell do you want us to do?' the furious Bradley demanded of Eisenhower's staff. 'Pull back and blow it up?' He later added bitterly, 'It always made me mad to have to beg for opportunities to win battles.' Montgomery likewise prevented Simpson's Ninth Army from crossing the Rhine at Düsseldorf, since his own setpiece attack was not scheduled for a further three weeks. The argument of Eisenhower, and of course Montgomery himself, was that the northern route into Germany offered incomparably better going for great armies than the central front. Yet

the plan had presumed serious German resistance. Given the new reality, that of German collapse, there is little doubt that caution could have been thrown to the winds, and the Allies might have embarked upon a headlong dash to meet the Russians by whatever corridors their spearheads could force open.

First Army fought a hard battle through the days following the capture of the bridge at Remagen, as the Germans threw everything they could muster into the struggle for its destruction: armour, frogmen, artillery, even a handful of surviving aircraft. The loss of Remagen cost von Rundstedt his job as Hitler's commander in the West, for the second and last time. He was replaced by Albert Kesselring, the Luftwaffe general now recalled from Italy where he had waged the most brilliant defensive campaign of the war since 1943. But even Kesselring could do little with the ruined armies he now inherited. The Remagen bridgehead steadily expanded, and its German attackers were easily crushed. Everywhere, the tide was rushing too rapidly over the breaches in the sandcastles of Hitler's defences for his surviving formations to perceive any hope of restoring them.

Patton used the period of delay before Montgomery's Rhine crossing to clear the western bank from Koblenz to Mannheim. On the

night of 22 March, his men crossed the river at Oppenheim, between Mainz and Mannheim. They met scant opposition. When Hitler demanded instant action to repel them, he was told that the means no longer existed. Just five newly-repaired tanks, at a depot 100 miles from the crossing, were available to roll west and challenge Patton's advance. Further north, the US 3rd Armoured Division entered Cologne on 5 March, awestruck by the great wasteland of rubble created by years of Allied bombing.

Montgomery began his massive crossing of the Rhine near Wesel on the night of 23 March, accompanied by a bombardment laid down by

The advancing Allied armies liberated thousands of prisoners of war of all nationalities, many of whom had spent five years in the German prison camps. Here, liberated Allied prisoners board C-47 transport planes for repatriation to their homelands.

3,000 guns and massed 'carpet-bombing'. The operation involved 59,000 British and American engineers. Amphibious tanks and infantry crossed the river and established bridgeheads with little difficulty. The way forward was cleared with an airborne drop, the last great parachute operation of the war, by two divisions. By 28 March, the bridgehead was twenty miles deep and thirty wide. Yet Montgomery refused to order a general advance until he had built up a force of twenty divisions and 1,500 tanks on the east bank. When at last his armies began to move forward, their principal impediment was not the German army, but the mountains of rubble in their path, brought down by bombing and shellfire.

On 7 April, in a freak act of warfare almost overlooked by historians, German Me-109 fighters undertook a massed suicide mission against American bomber formations over Hannover. Having

Top and above French colonial soldiers, veterans of five years of captivity.

Right British troops, including an airborne soldier distinguishable by his red beret, probably captured during the great Allied airborne operations of 1944.

despaired of challenging the Allied air armadas by conventional tactics, the Luftwaffe recruited 184 volunteer pilots to ram the Flying Fortresses in mid-air. In that day's action, 133 Me-109s were lost, with the lives of seventy-seven German pilots, for the destruction of twenty-three bombers. At this, its last gasp, the Nazi empire could still summon extraordinary reserves of fanaticism to mark its death throes.

An Indian Army soldier, probably captured during one of the many battles in North Africa from 1940 to 1942.

The Fall of the Third Reich

Thousands of German
soldiers in Frankenau, near
Kassel, after their capture
by the US First Army,
awaiting transport to the
nearest prisoner-of-war
camp.

DENMARK

BALTIC SEA

FLENSBURG

NORTH SEA

KIEL
Kiel Canal

RÜGEN

ROSTOCK

7 May

LÜBECK
SCHWERIN
WISMAR

STETTIN

WILHELMSHAVEN
EMDEN
GRONINGEN
OLDENBURG
BREMERHAVEN

HAMBURG
3 May

NEUSTRELITZ
STARGARD

18 Apr

BREMEN
28 Apr

DANNENBERG
DÖMITZ
WITTENBERG

Lüneburg
Heath
Belsen

Elbe

AMSTERDAM

Army Group 'H'
(Blaskowitz)

OSNABRÜCK
MINDEN

HANNOVER
10 Apr

TANGERMÜNDE

US Ninth Army

BERLIN
POTSDAM
FRANKFURT
KUSTRIN

NETHERLANDS
Twenty-fifth Army
ARNHEM

4 Apr

HAMELN

BRUNSWICK

G E R M A N Y

MÜNSTER
First Para Army
PADERBORN
LIPPSTADT

MAGDEBURG

Twelfth Army

BARBY
ROSSLAU

COTTBUS

Cdn First Army
(Crerar)
Br Second Army
(Dempsey)
WESEL
HAMM

Eleventh Army
BLANKENBURG
Harz Mts.
Brocken Pk

DESSAU
24 Apr

US Ninth Army
(Simpson)
ESSEN
DORTMUND
BOCHUM
Ruhr
WUPPERTAL

GÖTTINGEN
NORDHAUSEN

US First Army

HALLE

Leine
Saale

21 Army Group
(Montgomery)
DUISBURG
DÜSSELDORF
Sauerland
COLOGNE
Fifteenth Army

Army Group 'B'
(Model)

KASSEL
4 Apr

MERSEBERG
Buchenwald
WEISSENFELS

LEIPZIG

GÖRLITZ

Fifth Pz Army
BONN

MARBURG

ERFURT
GOTHA
WEIMAR
JENA

ZEITZ
COLDITZ

DRESDEN

Neisse

LIÈGE

REMAGEN
Sieg
Rhine

GIESSEN

OHRDRUF

Thuringian Forest

CHEMNITZ
USTI

BELGIUM
KOBLENZ
Lahn

FULDA
2 Apr
BAD ORB

US Third Army

Erzgebirge

PRAGUE

12 Army Group
(Bradley)
WIESBADEN

Seventh Army
HAMMELBURG
SCHWEINFURT

KARLOVY VARY

Seventh Army

US First Army
(Hodges)

FRANKFURT
HANAU

Spessart Mts

HOF

CZECHOSLOVAKIA

LUX
LUXEMBOURG
Moselle
TRIER

MAINZ
OPPENHEIM
US Third Army
(Patton)
ASCHAFFENBURG
Odenwald

WÜRZBURG
BAMBERG

BAYREUTH

PILSEN

WORMS
US Seventh Army
(Patch)
MANNHEIM

KITZINGEN
5 Apr

4 Apr
NÜREMBERG
20 Apr
FÜRTH

Bohemian Jura
CESKE
BUDEJOVICE
7 May

THIONVILLE
SAARBRÜCKEN

Army Group 'G'
(Hausser)

ANSBACH

18 Apr

Bohemian Forest
Vltava

6 Army Group
(Devers)
Neckar
HEILBRONN
Löwenstein Hills

REGENSBURG
26 Apr
US Seventh
Army

NANCY
Fr First Army
(de Lattre de Tassigny)
KARLSRUHE
4 Apr
PFORZHEIM
8 Apr
STUTTGART
ESSLINGEN
KIRCHHEIM

DONAUWORTH
INGOLSTADT

Danube

LINZ
5 May

STRASBOURG
Schwarzwald
TÜBINGEN

F Highland

DILLINGEN
First Army
AUGSBURG
Isar
LANDSHUT
30 Apr
LANDAU
PASSAU

US Third Army

F R A N C E
Nineteenth Army
Swabian Highland
ULM
23 Apr
EHINGEN
SIGMARINGEN

Dachau
LANDSBERG

MUNICH
30 Apr

Inn

BRAUNAU

SALZBURG
4 May

COLMAR
FREIBURG

Fr First Army
Lake Constance
MEMMINGEN
OBERAMMERGAU
FÜSSEN

US Seventh Army

ROSENHEIM

BERCHTESGADEN
4 May
Enns

BASEL

Schwarzwald
BREGENZ

Oberjoch
Pass

Fern
Pass
GARMISCH
PARTENKIRCHEN

KUFSTEIN

KITZBÜHEL

TAMSWEG

SWITZERLAND
Aarlberg
Pass
IMST

Resia
Pass

T y r
LANDECK

INNSBRUCK

A U S T R I A

Brenner
Pass
4 May

A L P S

KLAGENFURT

BOLZANO

I T A L Y

US Fifth Army

YUGOSLAVIA

▓	OCCUPIED BY ALLIED FORCES, 28 MARCH 1945
▰▰▰▶	BRITISH ATTACKS
━━▶	US ATTACKS
▷	FRENCH ATTACKS
▨	GERMAN POCKETS
░	OCCUPIED BY RUSSIAN FORCES, 16 APRIL
□	CONCENTRATION CAMPS

MILES 0 — 120
KILOMETRES 0 — 200

The Allied advance through Germany uncovered the horrors of war in the concentration camps. During April the Allies could have reached Berlin itself, but Eisenhower kept to his agreement that they would halt at the Elbe.

THE BOUNDARIES between the Eastern and Western Allies' zones of occupation in Germany had been fixed many months before the end of the war, and confirmed at the Yalta conference in February. The ailing Roosevelt, still deluded that he could do business with Stalin on terms compatible with Western interests, readily accepted Soviet arrangements for the future of Poland which effectively betrayed the very cause for which the West had gone to war. Yet from the Russian standpoint, there was a ruthless logic and justice about the political course that they now pursued in Eastern Europe. Since 1941 the Western Allies had made war on their own terms, and in their own time. They had delayed for more than two years a confrontation with the Germans in North-West Europe because they feared its cost. It was the Russian people, from beginning to end, who had borne the overwhelming burden of defeating the Nazis. They were now determined both to exact their revenge, in the form of reparations agreed at Yalta, and to guarantee their future security by assuming the hegemony over Eastern Europe from which they had deposed Germany.

These Wehrmacht soldiers seem pleased that they have become prisoners of the Americans and not the Russians.

In the spring of 1945, while the Germans were obsessed either with escape from the advancing Russian armies or with saving the greatest

A view of massed German prisoners boarding US lorries with the undamaged town of Frankenau in the background.

In April 1945, US First and Ninth Armies took 325,000 Germans prisoner at the end of the fighting for the Ruhr pocket, the largest single surrender by the Wehrmacht during the Second World War. This picture shows a German NCO leading his men to the lorries.

possible portion of their country from Soviet occupation, the Western Allies' knowledge that the post-war boundary was fixed denied their commanders a sense of urgency about pressing east. For Eisenhower to have dashed for Berlin with the intention of retaining the city, the British and American governments would have had to break their pact with Stalin. For all Churchill's impassioned rhetoric about the Nazi capital as a prize of victory, this was never plausible. Eisenhower declared repeatedly in those last weeks that Berlin was a mere map reference, of no strategic interest to him. In an important sense he was correct, though a commander of more imagination might have found irresistible the symbolic triumph of a last drive for the Nazi capital. Instead, however, the Supreme Commander allowed his energies to be distracted by the final great military delusion of the war: against all the evidence of absolute German collapse, he was persuaded that Hitler's armies were preparing for a last great stand in a 'National Redoubt' in Bavaria. To meet this mythical threat, he allowed the bulk of his forces to be diverted southwards, while his northern armies pursued a ponderous, almost leisurely course east to meet the Russians.

It had now become a matter of just anxiety among most men of the

The GIs who first encountered the Red Army on the River Elbe also came across escaping Allied prisoners of war. The Scottish soldier in the foreground was found making his way west by bicycle. George Stevens stands centre left, facing camera.

25 April 1945: US troops advancing from the West link-up with Soviet troops for the first time on the River Elbe. It soon became a publicity event.

Allied armies to survive this final phase and see victory. They were weary and embittered, as they probed cautiously up the roads of Germany in their Shermans and half-tracks, meeting pocket after pocket of fanatical resisters: teenagers manning *Panzerfaust* anti-tank rockets, fragments of SS units, old men pushed forward by local fanatics with rifles and grenades to make a last gesture of defiance for the Fatherland. At each such position, there was a brief explosion as a leading Allied vehicle 'brewed up', or was stopped in its tracks by an exploding mine. A deluge of Allied fire descended upon the defenders' position. If necessary, a fighter-bomber strike or artillery barrage was

called down to destroy it. Then the advancing column rolled on, sweeping contemptuously aside the barricades of farm carts and furniture, leaving only a handful of German and Allied corpses to mark an encounter that would enter no history books. It was a scene repeated day after day along the length of the Allied front. The local civilian population looked on in numbed dismay and apprehension at the ruin Nazism had brought upon their country. Most Germans were by now deeply relieved to see American and British forces overrun their towns and villages. They knew that they had thus gained safety from the Russians. The draconian non-fraternization orders issued by

Soviet troops, led by
Major-General Rusakov,
commander of the 58th
Guards Rifle Division,
already surrounded by
photographers as they
march towards their
meeting with American
troops from the US 69th
Infantry Division at Torgau.

American GIs were
surprised to see cavalry
units among the Soviet
troops, horses having been
phased out of American
service many years earlier.

the Allied commanders quickly proved honoured more by their breach than by their observance.

Patton, having gained rich laurels for his leadership in the winter battles, marred the last act of the war with a characteristic misjudgement. Early on 26 March, he detached a column of 300 men on his personal orders to liberate a prisoner-of-war camp, thirty-five miles north-east of his positions, at Hammelburg. He almost certainly knew, and was influenced by, the fact that his own son-in-law was one of the captives. After heavy fighting, the column reached the camp and sought to escape with some of the prisoners, though most sensibly elected to remain behind the wire. On their return journey, the Americans were fought to a standstill and obliged to abandon their vehicles. Just fifteen men of the task force fought their way back to the American lines, along with twenty-five prisoners excluding Patton's son-in-law, who was wounded in fighting at the camp. This was a

General Emil Reinhardt, commander of the US 69th Infantry Division, poses with Major-General Rusakov in a show of Allied solidarity.

American GIs found Russian women soldiers a welcome novelty. This GI loses no time in getting acquainted.

gratuitous fiasco of the kind which, again and again, was to dog Patton's career.

For those cities of Germany still awaiting the invading armies, the Allied bomber offensive continued to rain down mass death and destruction to the very end. Until the first months of 1945, the ruin of Germany's cities and the wholesale killing of civilians could be justified by the damage that was thus being done to Hitler's remaining war-making capacity. By the end of January 1945, however, the Nazis' gas, water, power and rail systems were in chaos. Fuel supplies on and off the battlefield were near to exhaustion. Railway signalling, telephones and industrial communications were almost extinct. Yet some of the most terrible mass destruction raids of the war took place in the weeks that followed, with the Luftwaffe reduced to near impotence, and the Allied air forces at the summit of their strength and technical skill. 'In Bomber Command we have always worked on the assumption that bombing anything in Germany is better than bombing nothing', said that steely Cromwellian, Sir Arthur Harris, Commander-in-Chief of Bomber Command. The airmen undertook the

Dresden raid on 13 February without any consciousness that it differed significantly from hundreds of others before it: 'The intentions of the attack,' declared Bomber Command's briefing notes to aircrew, 'are to hit the enemy where he will feel it most, behind an already partially collapsed front ... and incidentally to show the Russians when they arrive what Bomber Command can do.' Somewhere between 30,000 and 100,000 people died, and one of the most beautiful cities of Germany, of negligible industrial relevance, was obliterated. Berlin, Chemnitz, Leipzig and other towns suffered the same scale of attack in the weeks that followed. When protests developed in Britain following the destruction of Dresden, Harris dismissed them: 'I would not regard the whole of the remaining cities of Germany as worth the bones of one British grenadier', he wrote. 'The feeling over Dresden could easily be explained by any psychiatrist. It is connected with German bands and Dresden shepherdesses.' Area bombing of Germany's cities was halted only on 16 April.

By a ghastly irony, the bomber offensive was merely bringing upon Germany the same misery and destruction that her own leader had decreed for her. On 18 March, when Hitler's Armaments Minister Albert Speer urged Hitler that some steps should be taken to safeguard the means of survival and provision of vital services for the defeated Germans, he was appalled by the response: 'If the war is lost, the nation will also perish. This fate is inevitable', Hitler declared. 'There is no necessity to take into consideration the basis which the

Soviet soldiers put on an impromptu cabaret at Torgau. This Soviet dancer has a Nazi dagger tucked into his boot.

Two soldiers of the Red Army provide the music.

A typical Soviet soldier.
Unlike the American GIs,
Soviet soldiers often went
into battle without
helmets, but they wore
their medals in action.

Major-General Terry Allen
of the US 104th Infantry
Division, known as the
'Timberwolves', with
General Sohanov at
Delitzsch on 28 April.

people will need to continue a most primitive existence. On the contrary, it will be better to destroy these things ourselves because this nation will have proved to be the weaker one and the future will belong solely to the stronger eastern nation' – Russia. 'Besides, those who will remain after the battle are only the inferior ones, for the good ones have been killed.' At mortal risk, Speer devoted himself to frustrating Hitler's orders for the destruction of German industry. Even in those last days, the relentless purge of Hitler's enemies and critics continued, the bloody executions of officers who had taken part in the plot against him. While he himself lingered in the subterranean fantasy world of the Berlin *Führerbunker* with Bormann, Goebbels, Eva Braun and a few score staff officers and guards, his other acolytes were intriguing to supplant him, to make terms with their enemies for themselves and for Germany. Both Himmler and Göring made fanciful attempts to negotiate with the Allies.

While Montgomery's armies pushed north-east towards Bremen, Hamburg and the Baltic at Lübeck, the US Ninth and First Armies bypassed the Ruhr north and south. They linked at Lippstadt on 1 April, having encircled Model's Army Group B, the debris of twenty-one German divisions. Bradley allowed himself to make a serious error of judgement by diverting much of his strength to assault the entrapped Germans, whose fate was anyway sealed. Army Group B surrendered on 18 April, having merely inflicted a gratuitous eighteen

Watched by a woman refugee and her child, a Soviet soldier fires at escaping German troops fleeing westward across the River Elbe.

A common sight in the last days of the war were the freed Russian and Polish slave workers making their way home. These men worked in the *Mittelwerk* underground rocket factory at Niedersachsenwerfen, near Nordhausen, where 30,000 labourers from all over Europe were used in the Nazi V1 and V2 rocket programme. The camp was liberated by the US First Army in April 1945.

days of combat, casualties and delay on the American armies. Some 325,000 prisoners, including thirty generals, fell into American hands. Model shot himself, one of 101 German generals who committed suicide in the course of the Second World War. But even as Army Group B lay entrapped, American forces had swept on past them towards the Elbe, meeting negligible opposition. On the evening of 11 April, after advancing sixty miles in a single day, elements of Ninth Army reached the river near Magdeburg, and crossed the following day as Vienna fell to the Russians. American troops were now within sixty miles of Berlin. Further north, the Canadians were compelled to face some of the toughest resistance of this phase of the war as they fought through the innumerable canal and river crossings of northern Holland against a skilful German defence. They took Arnhem at last on 14 April, and broke through to the North Sea two days later. On the 16th also, as the US Seventh Army reached Nüremberg, Zhukov's armies broke out of their bridgeheads on the Oder. Sweeping through the last coherent German defences, they reached the outskirts of Berlin five days later.

On the afternoon of 25 April, a 26-man patrol from the US 69th Infantry Division led by Lieutenant Albert Kotzebue was probing cautiously through empty countryside west of the Elbe, searching for escaping Allied prisoners of war and surrendering Germans. Many houses were flying white flags, and their inhabitants nursed their silent fears behind closed doors. Kotzebue was shocked to encounter one farmhouse where an entire family sat dead around their kitchen table, having taken poison. A few miles on, close to the river in the village of Leckwitz, he saw a man riding a pony, wearing a uniform that he had never seen before. The American looked at the Russian. The Russian looked at the American. A Russian-speaker in the patrol asked the soldier where the rest of his unit was, and was told: 'On the Elbe.' At the river bank, Kotzebue and his men found a rowing boat.

They pushed themselves across the water using rifles as paddles. On the other side they were appalled to discover scores of dead civilians, men, women and children, sprawled among their carts and possessions. There was nothing to show how they had died, but it was not difficult to guess, with the Red Army at hand. Shortly afterwards, the American soldiers met the first group of Russians. Each side saluted the other without emotion or excitement. It was just after 1.30 pm.

Two young girls with their small cartload of belongings setting off on the long trek home.

But the meeting that history would officially record as the first link-up between Soviet and American troops occurred three hours later at Torgau, where Koniev's 58th Guards Rifle Division and the US First Army met to split the ruins of the Third Reich, seventy-five miles south of Berlin. The 69th Division's commander, General Reinhardt, was

The Kehlsteinhaüs stands
above the site of the
Berghof, Hitler's Bavarian
retreat. General
Eisenhower ordered his
forces to move south to
capture this area amid
rumours that a fanatic
group of Nazis was forming
a 'National Redoubt'.

Troops of the US Third
Army took Berchtesgaden
in the last week of April
1945. Here George Stevens
and Ivan Moffat pose in
front of the local post
office.

The entrance to the Bürger Bräu Keller in Munich where Hitler made his first speeches as leader of the Nazi party in the 1920s, and the scene of an attempt on his life on 8 November 1939.

initially furious with his own men for breaching their unit boundaries by driving to the Elbe. Then, when he understood that his formation would enjoy the glory of having made the first encounter with Stalin's armies, he swallowed his displeasure and drove forward to take part in the exchange of greetings between Allies. For all the much photographed show of friendship between the Russians and Anglo-Americans, it quickly became apparent that beneath the surface the Soviets cherished profound hostility and suspicion towards the men of Eisenhower's armies. Little warmth, or even civility, survived beyond the publicized encounters of the first few days.

Hitler and his surviving followers were now encircled in their last bastion. Their fantasies persisted to the end. When Roosevelt died on 12 April, Goebbels persuaded Hitler that this would prove a moment to match the Czarina's death, the salvation of Frederick the Great. The long-awaited collapse of the Grand Alliance must follow. 'Bring out

The Feldherrnhalle, Munich, showing the sarcophagi of the Nazi 'martyrs' who died in the *putsch* of 9 November 1923.

our best champagne!' demanded the Propaganda Minister. 'My Führer, I congratulate you! It is written in the stars that the second half of April will be the turning point for us. This is Friday, April the 13th.' Yet as the Russian artillery began to fire on Berlin, as their infantry began to fight street by street into the capital, even Goebbels and Hitler could no longer sustain their delusions. 'Poor, poor Adolf,' Eva Braun whimpered to the test pilot Hanna Reitsch, 'deserted by everyone, betrayed by all. Better that ten thousand die than he be lost to Germany.' In the early hours of 29 April, Hitler at last married Eva Braun, that most colourless and commonplace of great tyrants' lovers. That afternoon, they learned of Mussolini's death at the hands of Italian partisans. The German armies in Italy had surrendered unconditionally to the Allies. Hitler had his dogs shot, gave poison

General Patton's Third
Army rolled into western
Czechoslovakia during the
last weeks of the European
war. His advance was
halted not by Germans but
by General Eisenhower,
who ordered that the
territory east of Pilsen
should be taken by the
Soviet armies.

capsules to his secretaries with a word of apology that he could offer
no better parting gift. After saying farewell to his staff, on the
afternoon of 30 April he and his bride killed themselves, speedily
followed by Goebbels, and his wife, who first murdered their six
children. The bodies of Hitler and Eva Braun were burnt. Grand
Admiral Karl Dönitz was informed by radio signal that the Führer had
nominated him as his successor.

On the evening of 1 May, the *Führerbunker* in Berlin was set on fire,
and some five hundred of its occupants trickled away through the
streets and subway tunnels of Berlin to make their several attempts at
escape from the Russians. Many succeeded. Some, almost certainly
including Martin Bormann, died as they were caught in the street
fighting. The Russians took 100,000 prisoners when the last areas of

Berlin fell to them on 2 May. At 3.00 pm that day, as a great silence at last took over the city, Russian soldiers in their thousands burst into cheers and shouts in the streets, embracing each other, breaking out food and drink wherever they could find it. In more wretched fashion, they embarked upon an orgy of rape and looting unseen in scale in Western Europe since the Dark Ages. Yet to men who had survived what Stalin's soldiers had survived, it seemed the most meagre justice to seize whatever prizes they could discover in the ruins of the Third Reich. Even as they plundered Berlin, the investigators of SMERSH were picking over the ruins of the *Führerbunker*, intent on confirming whether Hitler had lived or died. Only after days of macabre confusion, amid so many wrecked buildings and half-incinerated corpses, were they confident that the German leader was gone forever.

In the last hours of Hitler's life, elements of the US First Army linked with the Russians at Eilenburg. Munich was occupied. The

On 30 April, as Soviet troops approached the *Führerbunker* in the centre of Berlin, Adolf Hitler and his new wife Eva Braun committed suicide. This trench in the garden of the Reich Chancellery is the probable site where their bodies were burnt after being sprinkled with petrol from jerry cans.

Allied armies in Italy met French troops on the Franco-Italian border. On 2 May, as Ireland's Prime Minister Eamon de Valera called at the German Legation in Dublin to express his condolences on the death of the Führer, the British Second Army reached the Baltic, securing Denmark from the Russians. German forces in Hamburg capitulated the next day. On 4 May, a million German troops in the Netherlands, Denmark and north-west Germany surrendered to the Allies. German representatives reached Rheims the next day to discuss final, overall surrender terms at Eisenhower's headquarters. Their purpose was to gain a few days' grace in which as many soldiers and civilians as possible could flee west out of the path of the Russians before all movement was checked. The Allies spurned their manoeuvrings. Germany surrendered unconditionally at 2.41 am on the morning of 7 May. The war in Europe was declared officially ended by President Truman and Prime Minister Churchill on 8 May, Victory in Europe

The graves of Soviet soldiers who fell in the battle for Berlin from 21 April to 2 May 1945. The Soviets suffered more than 300,000 casualties in the fighting for the Nazi capital.

George Stevens and fellow American officers inspect the ruins of the Reich Chancellery. This huge building in Berlin was repeatedly damaged by Allied bombing before being wrecked by the fighting in the city which ended on 2 May 1945.

In the struggle for the city an estimated 100,000 Berliners were killed. This picture shows a typical street scene in the days after the war.

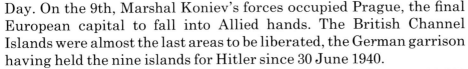

Day. On the 9th, Marshal Koniev's forces occupied Prague, the final European capital to fall into Allied hands. The British Channel Islands were almost the last areas to be liberated, the German garrison having held the nine islands for Hitler since 30 June 1940.

The destruction of German power in Europe had cost 586,628 American casualties, 135,576 of these killed, since 6 June 1944. The British, Canadians, French and other Allies lost 179,666 troops, including about 60,000 killed. Before the end of the campaign, 5,412,219 Allied troops had fought under Eisenhower's command, bringing with them a million vehicles and over eighteen million tons of supplies. The Russians sustained 304,887 casualties merely in the period between 16 April and 8 May, in the last battles of the war, extraordinary evidence of the share of sacrifice that they endured. In the same period, they lost 2,156 tanks and self-propelled guns and 527 aircraft. Germany was estimated to have lost some five million dead, military and civilian, since September 1939. The last battle for Berlin alone added 100,000 German civilians to the death toll. 'By the most conservative calculation,' the outstanding historian of the Red Army Professor John Erickson has written, 'the battle for Berlin thus cost half a million human beings their lives, their well-being or their sanity.' Hitler's empire was broken at last amid destruction, misery and slaughter on the satanic scale that he himself had deemed appropriate.

Few buildings in Berlin escaped destruction as this view, with the Reichstag in the background, shows.

DACHAU

Ten miles north of Munich a signpost points to the Dachau concentration camp in one direction, SS barracks in the other.

Allied troops were appalled by the spectacle that greeted them when they reached the Nazi concentration camps like Dachau. This victim appears to have been killed only hours before the liberation of Dachau camp on 29 April 1945.

Among the gruesome
sights awaiting American
troops was this stack of
emaciated corpses, waiting
to be taken to the
crematorium.

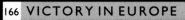

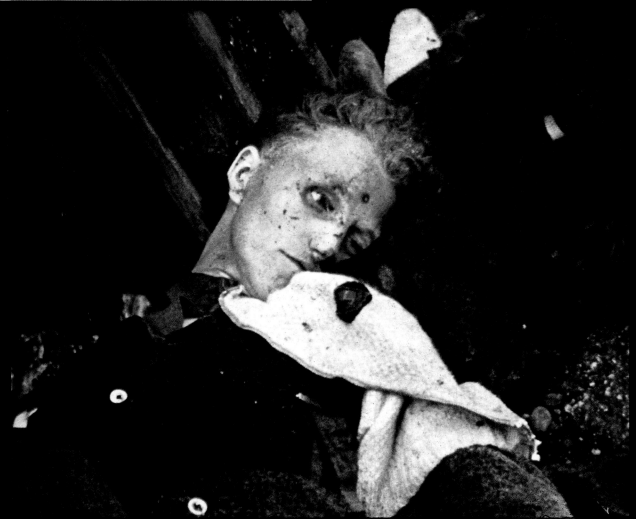

In many instances German troops taken prisoner in or near the concentration camps were killed on the spot by Allied troops and former inmates unable to contain their rage.

An immediate task was the feeding of starving survivors. Here a cartload of bread is unloaded at the camp.

Newly-liberated
concentration camp
inmates cook themselves a
meal.

Typhus was rife in all
liberated concentration
camps. Here inmates are
being deloused with DDT
powder.

The inmates of the camps
were of all ages. These two
young boys, walking along
the Lagerstrasse in Dachau,
still wear their striped
concentration-camp
uniforms.

Many of the inmates were
barely alive when the

At the camp hospital, inmates are seen alongside one of their comrades who did not survive to see the camp liberated.

The SS barracks, Dachau.

Some of the German guards
disguised themselves as
inmates in a bid to escape.
As this picture shows, their
well-fed faces give them
away.

A freed inmate inspects a
line of German prisoners
for possible war criminals.

German prisoners being interrogated by a US officer.

The tables are turned. These German prisoners, eyed by freed inmates, ponder their fate.

The Aftermath

The roads of central Europe
were filled with refugees
after the war. These
Russian forced labourers
are seen returning to their
homeland from
Czechoslovakia.

ALMOST THE only public act of Dönitz's brief imposture as Germany's Führer was his radio broadcast on the night of 1 May 1945, in which he advanced the grotesque deceit that Hitler had died 'a hero's death', declared his determination to save his country from Bolshevism, and concluded by assuring the German people that 'God will not forsake us after so much suffering and sacrifice.' It was remarkable how frequently the Nazi leadership invoked the Deity in their latter days. In reality, Dönitz's absurd rump government, which had been established at Flensburg on the Danish border, was dissolved by the Allies on 23 May 1945. The bleak Grand Admiral and all his colleagues were arrested, and most served terms of imprisonment after the Nüremberg war crimes trials. Himmler was captured attempting an escape to Bavaria through the Anglo-American lines disguised as an army private. He took poison during an interrogation on 23 May. Göring lived to stand trial at Nüremberg, where he defended himself with dignity and skill, and committed suicide on the eve of his execution as a last jest against his captors. Of the lesser Nazis a few were hanged, many more were imprisoned, and yet more escaped. Perhaps partly

Thousands of Poles who had served with Polish forces in Britain and elsewhere under British control were allowed to return to Poland if they so chose. This picture shows one such group being repatriated at Lübeck in July 1945.

These British, Russian and Polish officers seem to have found a common language.

Berlin was divided into Soviet, American, British and French sectors. The Brandenburg Gate was the demarcation line between the Soviet and British sectors of the city. In the background are the remains of the Unter den Linden, one of the most fashionable streets in pre-war Berlin.

The Soviet red star soon tooks its place on the skyline of battered Berlin.

because many of the Western Allied leaders felt uneasy sitting in joint judgement upon Germany's great criminals alongside the Russians, with their own terrible record of bloodshed, the victors' judgements upon the vanquished remained remarkable for their forbearance.

Half Europe seemed to be moving along its roads that summer of 1945: forced labourers and deportees struggling to return to their homes; soldiers of the Wehrmacht and the SS making desperate, epic attempts to escape from the Russians or war crimes investigators, fleeing to their homes or beyond the reach of Allied justice; refugees displaced by bombing or ground action searching for shelter; widows and orphans bereft of family and possessions looking for the means with which to support life. As late as 10 May, the Russians complained bitterly to Eisenhower that German soldiers were still fighting Russians in their efforts to break through westwards and surrender to the Anglo-Americans.

All these prisoners and victims the Allied armies were compelled to examine, to control, to feed, where necessary to imprison or care for. The history of the period was eternally sullied by the Allies' forcible return of almost two million Russians in the Anglo-American zones. Many had fought in German uniform either under compulsion, or driven by bitter resentment that their own nations had been in- corporated in the Soviet Union against their wishes. Some were forced labourers, some Jews, some exiles. None wished to return east, yet all were condemned to do so by Western agreement with Stalin at Yalta. Most Allied soldiers detested the part that they were compelled to play, transhipping endless truck- and trainloads of men at bayonet point, most of whom knew that they were returning to die, and some of whom preferred to do so by their own hands.

An all-women workforce was conscripted to clear the rubble of Berlin once the war was over, their menfolk being either dead or prisoners of war.

As this picture shows, some spirit still remained among the conquered Berliners.

Yet the most horrendous burden facing the Allies was that of tending the surviving inmates of the concentration camps. Shocked American troops had liberated Dachau on 29 April, after a brief battle with an SS rearguard. They found 'freight cars full of piled cadavers ... bloody heaps at the rail car doors where weakened prisoners, trying to get out, were machine-gunned to death ... rooms stacked almost to the ceiling high with tangled human bodies ...' The scenes were repeated at Belsen, Buchenwald, Ravensbrück and all the other Nazi industrialized mass murder plants. Most of the survivors were too shocked and broken even to comprehend their deliverance. Those who did so sought terrible and summary revenge upon their former guards, indeed any uniformed German within their reach. A British nurse caring for some of the former inmates in a military hospital wrote: 'The dead eyes rarely kindled a response ... Although the patients had the freedom to wander at will within the compounds of the hospital, they were always back in the ward at mealtimes, no matter where they had strayed, silently converging on the food trolley with their tin plates, eyes rivetted on the containers full of meat and vegetables. The helpings had to be small at first, for their shrunken stomachs could not take normal rations. Despite the regular meals,

Sister Davies and I would find, while making the beds, a slice of corned beef, a potato or a piece of bread hidden under a pillow, for they could not yet be sure that another day would bring more food. Sometimes we despaired for these men. What future was there for them? No one knew where their families were and they seemed to have forgotten that they ever had wives or children. They only cared for the food trolley. Every other instinct or emotion had been suppressed except the will to survive.'

Eisenhower set up his headquarters in the former I.G.Farben building in Frankfurt, and set about the rigid enforcement of Allied non-fraternization orders. In the words of his biographer: 'His hatred of the Germans was wide-ranging and ran very deep. He definitely wanted them punished, humiliated, made to pay. He blamed the Germans for starting the war and for prolonging it.' Yet even after the terrible revelations of the concentration camps, the six million Jews killed, many Allied soldiers found it difficult to sustain their hostility

The Soviet sector of Berlin in July 1945. The work of reconstruction meant demolishing the shells of many shattered buildings.

The collapse of the German
economy gave rise to a vast
black market involving
conqueror and conquered
alike. This picture shows
black marketeers in Berlin
after their arrest by
German police.

A Soviet poster showing
the chains binding Europe
being severed by British,
American and Soviet
swords – a symbol of inter-
Allied amity.

A Soviet military policewoman on point duty in Berlin, directing the traffic with some style.

A wounded survivor walks past a wrecked tank near the Reichstag building, a reminder of the bitter fighting for Berlin in April and May 1945.

to the Germans in the pitiful circumstances of their defeat. The victors were weary of killing, and tired of fear and bitterness, propaganda and national causes. Patton was foremost among those who expressed a further, as yet unfashionable, view: that the defeated Germans posed a lesser threat to the West than its erstwhile Allies, the Russians. Then Patton went further, and publicly expressed his reluctance to join the hunt for former Nazis: 'The Nazi thing is just like a Democratic and Republican election fight.' Eisenhower had had enough. With the end of the war, Patton's indispensability as a battlefield commander was at an end. Eisenhower relieved him of his command of Third Army. It was a sad conclusion to a remarkable military career.

From the moment of the surrender, the government of Germany posed an enormous problem for the Allies. In 1918, the entire bureaucracy, the fabric of authority in the country, had been left intact by the victors. In 1945, policy decreed that Nazis must be banished from all positions in the bureaucracy and in government. At a stroke, the controlling forces of the nation were almost eliminated. A long-prepared, yet at once overstretched, structure of Allied military government replaced it. Germany entered the sordid, gloomy postwar era of hunger and the black market; of families picking over mountains of rubble for salvage; Allied officers and men making a twilight living selling petrol, tyres, cigarettes; widespread prostitution; men and women of all nationalities urgently seeking papers, any papers or identity documents that would enable them to cross a frontier, purchase food, or lose a past. Throughout much of Europe the age of Graham Greene's *Third Man* had come, and was to persist for half a decade.

A Soviet hoarding on the East-West axis in central Berlin depicts the Allied war leaders – Churchill, Roosevelt and Stalin – at Yalta.

On 1 July 1945, the Allied armies began to withdraw behind the boundaries of the occupation zones agreed before Yalta. For the British and Americans, this involved large-scale movements of men across great distances. The four-party occupation of Berlin was secured across the Russian zone by a 20-mile-wide air corridor, and a road and railway link. The Russians rapidly began the systematic plundering of their own zone, the removal of vast quantities of industrial plant to their homeland. While the Allied armies were under strict order to take no food from the western zones where the local inhabitants were already in desperate need of it, the Red Army in eastern Germany lived ruthlessly off the land.

On 15 July, the last great conference of the war – for the struggle

British and Russian soldiers sightseeing at the ruins of the Reichstag in July 1945.

The Soviets were quick to build monuments to remind their fellow Allies and the conquered Germans that Soviet troops were the first to enter Berlin. The first Soviet tank to advance through the city was placed on this memorial plinth, seen here still under construction.

continued against Japan – took place between the Allied powers in Potsdam. In its midst, on 26 July, Churchill learned that his government had been defeated in Britain's first General Election in a decade. It was Clement Atlee who returned to Britain's seat at the conference table. The agreement that finally emerged from Potsdam, committing the Allies to uniform treatment of their respective zones of Germany, was the last for which they achieved joint consent for years to come. The common peace treaty with Germany which they pledged themselves to prepare was never attained. The East-West occupation boundaries of Germany became the frontier of the two post-war German nations. The ending of the war with Japan on 15 August 1945, following the dropping of the atomic bombs on Hiroshima and Nagasaki, passed almost unnoticed in the defeated land where Hitler's people prepared to face a winter of near-starvation without coal to heat their homes, without adequate shelter or clothing, amid absolute lack of employment except in vital services.

Yet if the anticlimax that followed V-E Day, the first frosts of the Cold War and the descent of the Iron Curtain, seemed a bitter ending to the great Allied 'crusade for democracy', the lasting fruits of victory were much less bitter. For all the odium heaped upon the division of

A mixed detachment of male and female Soviet soldiers marching in Berlin. The hotch-potch nature of the unit, of varying age groups, nationalities and uniforms, belies the fighting prowess of the Red Army.

Men of the three conquering nations: on the left two British RAF servicemen, in the centre a Soviet soldier and on the right two American officers at the Wannsee, a fashionable Berlin lakeside resort in the summer of 1945.

Germany between East and West, in their hearts most democrats in the Western World came to believe that partition had at last solved 'the German problem', the century-old threat to the stability of Europe. Most of those who had fought returned home to demobilization cherishing the knowledge that the Second World War had not been 'just another war', but a genuine struggle to defeat a great evil. When Zhukov came to Frankfurt in the late summer of 1945, Eisenhower played host at a banquet for the Russian marshal, perhaps more than any other one man the victor of the struggle against Germany. The Supreme Commander declared with justice in his speech afterwards: 'This war was a holy war, more than any other in history this war has been an array of the forces of evil against those of righteousness.' History has thus far endorsed his verdict, and acknowledged V-E Day as a just moment for celebration among the nations of the West.

Bibliography

Ambrose, S. E., *The Supreme Commander: The War Years of General Dwight D. Eisenhower*, Doubleday, New York, 1970

Aron, R., *De Gaulle Triumphant*, Putnam, New York, 1964

Belchem, D., *Victory in Normandy*, Chatto & Windus, London, 1981

Blumenson, Martin, *The Patton Papers 1940–1945*, Houghton Mifflin Co., Boston, 1974

Bradley, Omar, *A Soldier's Story*, Henry Holt & Co., New York, 1951

Bryant, Arthur, *Triumph in the West: 1943–1946*, Collins, London, 1959

Collins, J. Lawton, *Lightning Joe, An Autobiography*, Baton Rouge, Louisiana, 1979

Cooper, Matthew, *The German Army: Its Political and Military Failure*, Macdonald & Jane, London, 1978

Erickson, John, *The Road to Berlin*, Weidenfeld & Nicolson, London, 1983

Golley, John, *The Big Drop*, Janes, London, 1982

de Guingand, Frederick, *Operation Victory*, Hodder & Stoughton, London, 1947

Hamilton, Nigel, *Montgomery: The Making of a General*, 2 vols., Hamish Hamilton Ltd., London, 1981

Hastings, Max, *Bomber Command*, Michael Joseph, London, 1979; *Overlord*, Michael Joseph, London, 1984

Liddell Hart, Basil, *The Second World War*, Cassell, London, 1970

MacDonald, Charles B., *The Battle of the Bulge*, Weidenfeld & Nicolson, London, 1984

McBryde, Brenda, *A Nurse's War*, Chatto & Windus, London, 1979

Ryan, Cornelius, *The Last Battle*, Simon and Schuster, New York, 1966

Scott, Desmond, *Typhoon Pilot*, Secker & Warburg, London, 1982

Taylor, A. J. P., *The Second World War, An Illustrated History*, Hamish Hamilton Ltd., London, 1975

Wilmot, Chester, *The Struggle for Europe*, Harper & Bros, New York, 1952

Index